Process Drama and Multiple Literacies

Process Drama and Multiple Literacies

ADDRESSING SOCIAL, CULTURAL, AND ETHICAL ISSUES

Edited by
Jenifer Jasinski Schneider,
Thomas P. Crumpler, and
Theresa Rogers

HEINEMANN
Portsmouth, NH

Heinemann
A division of Reed Elsevier Inc.
361 Hanover Street
Portsmouth, NH 03801–3912
www.heinemanndrama.com

Offices and agents throughout the world

© 2006 by Heinemann

All rights reserved. No part of this book may be reproduced in any form or by any electronic or mechanical means, including information storage and retrieval systems, without permission in writing from the publisher, except by a reviewer, who may quote brief passages in a review.

The author and publisher wish to thank those who have generously given permission to reprint borrowed material:
On page 90, "Mobile Street Looking South" (M351-364) by Herbert Randall Jr. Black & White photograph, 1964. From Freedom Summer Photographs Collection. With kind permission from Herbert Randall Jr. and The University of Southern Mississippi Libraries, McCain Library and Archives, Hattiesburg, Mississippi.

Library of Congress Cataloging-in-Publication Data
Process drama and multiple literacies : addressing social, cultural, and ethical issues / edited by Jenifer Jasinski Schneider, Thomas P. Crumpler, and Theresa Rogers.
  p. cm.
Includes bibliographical references.
ISBN 0-325-00783-7 (alk. paper)
 1. Drama in education. I. Schneider, Jenifer Jasinski. II. Crumpler, Thomas P. III. Rogers, Theresa.
PN3171.P76 2006
371.39'9—dc22   2005030505

Editor: Lisa A. Barnett
Production service: Matrix Productions, Inc.
Production coordination: Patricia Adams
Typesetter: TechBooks
Cover design: Joni Doherty
Manufacturing: Steve Bernier

Printed in the United States of America on acid-free paper

10 09 08 07 06 VP 1 2 3 4 5

Contents

Acknowledgments   vii

Foreword
   Cecily O'Neill   ix

Introduction
   Thomas P. Crumpler, Theresa Rogers, Jenifer Jasinski Schneider   xiii

1. Educational Drama as Response to Literature:
   Possibilities for Young Learners
   Thomas P. Crumpler   1

2. Story Drama Structures:
   Building Supports for Multiple Literacies
   Juliana Saxton and Carole Miller   15

3. The *Antigone* Project:
   Using Drama and Multiple Literacies to Support Print
   Literacy Among Youth
   Kari-Lynn Winters, Theresa Rogers, and Andrew Schofield   35

4. Identity and Imagination of Immigrant Children:
   Creating Common Place Locations in Literary Interpretation
   Carmen L. Medina   53

5. "I'm a lot like her":
   Entering the World of *Others* Through Process Drama
   Karen S. Kelley   71

6. Full Circling:
   How Visual Literacy, Narrative Texts, and Students' Imaginations
   Turned Urban Fifth-Graders into Architects of History
   Trisha Wies Long   89

7. "Always Listen to Children":
Process Drama as a Site for Fostering Freedom, Voice, and Choice
Jenifer Jasinski Schneider   107

8. The Dilemma of the Bystander:
Using Literature, Art, Drama, and Poetry to
Deepen Understanding
Carmen Córdova   123

9. Drama, Diversity, and Children:
The Art and Ethics of Advocating for More than One
Beth Murray   139

Appendix: Drama and Multiple Literacy Structures and Strategies   155
Editors   159
Contributors   161

Acknowledgments

This book is a compilation of the work, teaching, and research of numerous classroom teachers and university researchers who have found ways to make learning meaningful for children. Through their imaginative, challenging, and innovative work with process drama, children are beginning to learn differently, think differently, and know differently.

We are indebted to Cecily O'Neill who introduced all of us to process drama as a tool for education. Her insight, challenges, and instruction on drama structures and possibilities have forever changed the way we view teaching and learning.

Jenifer and Theresa would also like to thank their husbands (Troy and Rob) and their children, Bethany and Mary / Shaun and Christopher, for all of the drama, process or otherwise, they bring to our lives. Of course we are always thankful for their unending support and love. Tom would like to thank his wife Kay for her love, support, and belief in the value of dramatic work as play. He is also thankful for his sons Dillon and Peter who do provide more drama than they know.

Foreword

Cecily O'Neill

For John Dewey, the continuing reconstruction of experience was at the heart of effective education. Writing in 1916, he insisted that nothing had brought pedagogical theory into greater dispute than did equating education with the provision of recipes and model lessons to teachers.[i] The methods outlined in this book have nothing to do with such reductive tactics. Instead, they aim at reconstructing the experience of students through powerful and generative approaches to learning. Built on sound theoretical foundations, this rich pedagogy engages students in multiple literacies expressed through various forms of representation. Process drama is a key element in these experiences, but almost every other art medium is involved. Alternative sign systems promote diverse ways of making meaning and elicit an impressive range of student responses requiring the exercise of their literary, visual, and dramatic imaginations.

Imagination is central to this kind of pedagogy. Although it is a necessary condition for almost all intellectual activity, imagination is insufficiently acknowledged as a powerful catalyst for learning. Where imagination is encouraged, a range of learning possibilities is immediately made available in the classroom. Speculation, interpretation, evaluation, and reflection, all demanding cognitive activities, are promoted. Opportunities arise for both teacher and students to make the kinds of personal, social, and curricular connections that transcend the traditional boundaries of the curriculum.

The innovative teachers whose work is so convincingly presented in these chapters invite their students to reflect imaginatively on a range of classic and contemporary texts. As they encounter the questions raised by these texts, the students enter into a dialogue with them and are challenged to bring the texts alive in their own minds. In work based on

---

[i] John Dewey, 1916. *Democracy and Education. An Introduction to the Philosophy of Education* (New York: Free Press, 1966), 170.

The Watsons Go to Birmingham—1963, we meet students in a multiage elementary class who use their own experience of family life to take on the perspectives and tensions of a fictional family and another ethnicity.[ii]

The imaginations and understanding of these students have been enlisted in what Eco has called "a performance of meaning under the guidance of the text." For Eco, every reception of a text is both an interpretation and a performance because in every reception the work takes on a fresh perspective.[iii] Responding to the promptings of the original, these students generate their own "texts" through writing, drawing, movement, drama, and film. Each of these responses invites further reflection, and their offerings are immediately validated and amplified by their teachers. We see the students modify their perspectives on the original, and begin to rewrite the text of the work within the text of their own lives.[iv] In Chapter 4, students who are themselves recent immigrants take on "the mantle of the expert" in response to a task set by the superintendent of the school district and work to develop a document aimed at helping new immigrants face the challenges they may meet in school. Generating these reflective "texts" requires that the students hold two realities in their minds. They place their imagined worlds inside the real world of their classrooms, constructing "common place locations" where imagination and reality are blurred.[v]

Maxine Greene, whose work has influenced many of the teachers in this book, regards education through the arts as an initiation into new ways of seeing, hearing, feeling, and moving. It signifies for her the nurture of a special kind of reflectiveness and expressiveness, a reaching out for meanings, a learning to learn.[vi] Greene insists that in order to test out new forms of social order and reflect on their moral implications, young people need opportunities to project themselves into rich hypothetical worlds.

This book is full of hypothetical worlds arising from significant texts and from the imaginations of all the participants. The teachers in these pages know that if their students are to become independent thinkers,

---

[ii] Karen S. Kelley, *"I'm a lot like her": Entering the World of Others Through Process Drama* (Chapter 5).

[iii] U. Eco, 1984. *The Role of the Reader: Explorations in the Semiotics of Texts* (Bloomington, IN: Indiana University Press), 49.

[iv] Roland. Barthes, 1980. *The Pleasure of the Text* (NY: Hill and Wang), 101.

[v] Carmen L. Medina, *Identity and Imagination of Immigrant Children: Creating Common Place Locations in Literary Interpretation* (Chapter 4).

[vi] Maxine Greene, 2001. *Variations on a Blue Guitar: The Lincoln Center Institute Lectures on Aesthetic Education* (NY: Teachers College Press), 188.

they must help them engage in the kinds of endeavors that will encourage serious critical insights into the society in which they live. If the students are unable to imagine things differently and consider the world from unfamiliar perspectives, they will be unable to bring about any change in their circumstances. The arts, and drama in particular, have always provoked these shifts of perspective. In taking on roles and projecting into problematic "as if" situations, students' assumptions are tested and their values scrutinized. The assumptions of the fifth-grade students in Chapter 8 as they investigate the roles of perpetrators and victims of oppression are re-evaluated when they come to the conclusion that bystanders who do not act to prevent injustice become perpetrators of oppression themselves.[vii]

It becomes obvious from all of the examples in this book that participation in aesthetic experience is always voluntary. It may serve instrumental purposes but can never be entirely subordinated to them. Aesthetic experience is likely to develop an unpredictable life of its own. True participation in both art and learning evokes independent thought, imaginative freedom, and a commitment to one's own ideas, but individual responses are modified by the recognition of the constraints of the context and by a growing responsibility to the group's efforts. Students involved in a courtroom drama dealing with the future of the abducted animal in *Shiloh* determine that the dog belongs to its abusive owner because "he paid for it" until one child, obeying a higher moral imperative, forces the others to reconsider their decision by insisting that "this trial isn't about money—it's about love."[viii]

The approaches proposed in this book are essentially inclusive. They build community. Social capacities are strengthened as students encounter one another in new roles, situations, and groupings. Though individual challenges and successes will arise, students are encouraged to think of themselves as people who might be able to work together to bring about justice and tolerance in their personal lives and in society. It is possible that the effects of the work described here may reach out beyond these classrooms and schools.

These profoundly courageous teachers and researchers will be an inspiration to others. Each of them is prepared to go beyond the prescribed goals, limited pedagogy, and restricted curricula that characterize too many classrooms. They understand that their ambitious

---

[vii]Carmen Cordóva, *The Dilemma of the Bystander: Using Literature, Art, Drama, and Poetry to Deepen Understanding* (Chapter 8).
[viii]Cordóva, *The Dilemma of the Bystander* (Chapter 8).

teaching objectives may not always be met in the ways they had anticipated. They are willing to deal with the unexpected. They take risks and are not afraid of failure. They choose texts and topics as locations of possibility, and for their openness to imaginative transformation and their potential for inviting students into active engagement with the work. The teachers bring *themselves* into the classroom as creative human beings while they build classroom communities that give students a voice in their own learning.

Above all, these gifted teachers respect and value their students as people. They work to offer opportunities for their students to grow as competent and complete individuals accepting responsibility for the society in which they live. The student who explored issues of betrayal, social status, and suicide in *Antigone* was reaching toward an understanding of this kind of responsibility when he produced this poetic fragment:

> *I will not tiptoe through life to arrive safely at death.*
> *Life lives in your blood, not your bullet.*
> *Love lives in your heart, not in your battle.*
> *Through my heart I feel and cry.*
> *Through your smile I learn to fly.*[ix]

[ix]Kari-Lynn Winters, Theresa Rogers, and Andrew Schofield, *The Antigone Project: Using Drama and Multiple Literacies to Support Print Literacy Among Youth.* (Chapter 3).

Introduction

Thomas P. Crumpler, Theresa Rogers, Jenifer Jasinski Schneider

The vistas of process drama and literacy continue to shift as we gain deeper insights into the complexity of how learners rehearse and construct meaning. These rehearsals and constructions challenge our understanding of what constitutes a text, how we read and interpret multimodal images and signs, and how we compose and design artifacts that include linguistic, oral, and visual sign systems. As teachers and students seek to broaden these understandings in the context of "multiple literacies" (learning across a range of print and nonprint genres and media) and as part of an increasingly global society, process drama has emerged as a promising approach for exploring the multifaceted nature of literacy learning.

Conceptually, process drama draws on the theories of language learning of Vygotsky (1978), Bruner's work in narrative as a paradigmatic structure for organizing experience (1986, 1990), Bateson's notion of the importance of play in learning processes (1955, 1973), and other scholarship situated in sociocultural views of learning. Further, process drama is linked to the tradition of educational drama that began in the United Kingdom late in the nineteenth century and continues to flourish throughout the world today (Bolton 1998). Process drama is, as O'Neill has argued, "a mode of learning" that allows learners of any age to use imagined roles to "explore issues, events, and relationships (O'Neill & Lambert 1983, 11). Process drama has evolved out of the work of Dorothy Heathcote, Gavin Bolton, Cecily O'Neill, and others who were interested in developing ways to activate learners' imaginations by using dramatic structures associated with a larger theatrical field to explore content area curriculum, texts, relationships readers have with texts, issues connected to texts, and other aspects of literacy learning in diverse educational settings.

Dorothy Heathcote's pioneering work in educational drama, beginning in the 1950s in England and continuing today, has had a profound effect on the field of classroom drama both in the United Kingdom and

North America (Bolton 1998). Her unique approach, which she labeled "mantle of the expert," is a complex pedagogy that uses "teacher in role" to facilitate and deepen learning with drama. Heathcote developed a way of building curriculum around drama work that she made look deceptively easy; however, it required careful planning, flexible implementation, and commitment to long-term learning goals (Heathcote & Bolton 1995). The structures of teacher in role, tableau, writing in role, and other terms essential for process drama have their origin in the work of Dorothy Heathcote.

O'Neill's scholarship is critical for understanding process drama, because she has been its most eloquent and thoughtful theorist. In the introduction to the book that conceptualized a framework for process drama (1995), O'Neill argued that process drama developed in the 1980s as a pedagogy that was different from more improvisational approaches to classroom drama, yet was also informed by a tradition of theater. The result was an approach that opened instructional space for teachers who were willing to de-center themselves in classrooms and participate in drama as learning with their students. In such classrooms, teachers and students might use process drama to respond to a work of fiction in the curriculum, explore issues and ideas that emerge from classroom discussion, delve more deeply into literature through reading and writing in role, and pursue numerous other possibilities where learners enact meaning. Process drama is primarily social, because it is realized in the company of others and involves negotiation and renegotiation of meaning as participants interpret and reinterpret their own views in concert with participants in a drama sequence. To put it another way, it uses the real to inform the fictional and the fictional to inform the real, and balances both to enrich cognitive and affective learning (Courtney 1995). In summary, process drama is a tool for learning, and, used effectively, it offers a way to mediate and focus the multiple sign systems that inform literacy development.

For example, if we were to use process drama as an instructional tool to explore a literary text such as *The Watsons Go to Birmingham—1963* (see Chapter 5 in this volume), we might invite students to consider the relationships among characters through use of a teacher in role as one of the family members, who talks with the students about issues raised by this story. Further, we might place students in role as characters that could be in the story and ask them to journal as those characters. Next we might ask students to create a tableau, a frozen silent moment of human figures, that attempts to capture and extend some aspect of that writing, and then we might ask students to choose a melody or song that could serve as a musical caption to that tableau. This sequence of process drama structures is not designed to create a play, although it draws on theater as both a conceptual and practical source. Rather, the goal is to begin creation of what O'Neill called "drama worlds" (1995) where learners can bring together personal, cultural, linguistic, musical, gestural, and other meaning systems and literacies to delve more deeply into relationships between the real and the fictional. It is provocative and potentially transformative work.

Conceptualizing an edited volume on the relationships between process drama and multiple literacies has been a provocative learning experience that has challenged us to explore and expand our thinking, teaching, and learning through drama. It has challenged us to reimagine the work of teaching and learning in schools, as so many stakeholders (parents, educators, politicians, and others) are concerned about testing, standards, and accountability, and so many others are concerned with school violence, racism, and character education. Schools must find new ways to educate students across multiple domains and contexts while also creating informed citizens who are respectful and thoughtful individuals. Process drama offers a possible solution to this challenge because it is a method for learning and teaching that can be used to integrate the content of numerous curricular areas while also developing the minds and the social consciences of students. Process-drama techniques allow students to view the world from multiple perspectives, involving them in situations in which they must make informed decisions and live with the consequences of their actions. Therefore, process drama is an educational tool for learning, thinking, and doing.

In this book we see drama as central to multiple literacy practices. Current theory and approaches to "multiliteracies" (e.g., Cope and Kalantzis 2000) often underestimate the power of the arts to support learners to move within "the increasing multiplicity and integration of meaning making" (p. 5)—a multiplicity that is evolving on an increasingly global stage. We feel that K–12 teachers can take that stage in classrooms with their students and use process drama as an educational tool to navigate the terrain of multiple literacies, which incorporates drama and other art forms into the process of rich multimodal meaning making. In fact, process drama has been documented as a tool for educating children across content areas and supporting their development in multiple literacies (see Wagner 1998). We have included chapters that articulate conceptual bases of process drama and connect it with other practices involving multiple literacies, as well as demonstrate the mutually enriching relationship between process drama and theater.

OVERVIEW OF CHAPTERS

The chapters in this book present a theoretical orientation that recognizes the shifting nature of literacy away from a single view of literacy toward multiple literacies. Further, the chapters demonstrate how the practices of process drama facilitate the development of multiple literacies and multiple perspectives with diverse learners. Each contributing author discusses critical, multiple literacies issues and how they can be addressed through process drama work.

Structuring classroom drama for explorations in multiple literacies

We begin with Tom Crumpler's chapter, in which he develops the theoretical foundation for a dramatic model of response to literature. Crumpler asserts that a dramatic model of reading response provides structures that help readers to question, critique, and evaluate the texts they are interacting within terms of the dynamics of power. Tom clearly explicates the ways in which process drama parallels the acts of reading and interpreting texts in that readers and drama participants position themselves with/against characters, process information, manipulate contextual factors, monitor their understanding, and engage in reflection. Next, Juliana Saxton and Carole Miller present their work with a particular story drama structure that offers students "opportunities to work with the multiple 'languages' that effective literacies explore." They suggest ways to delve into what they call "self-literacy," whereby learners gain insights into how multiple meaning systems shape their own identities. Saxton and Miller provide specific structures for teachers who are interested in using drama to uncover what their students are hearing, seeing, and doing with literacy as well as what lies *underneath*. Then Kari-Lynn Winters, Theresa Rogers, and Andrew Schofield present their work with struggling youth. Through drama structures in their "Antigone project," which interwove multiple literacy forms, a group of adolescents received additional opportunities to improve their composing, decoding, comprehending, and revising skills, while emphasizing the negotiations of their social relationships and drawing on their cultural experiences to comment upon and critique multiple texts. Winters, Rogers, and Schofield highlight the stories of three adolescent males who maneuvered through drama spaces in individual ways to make sense of literacy and textual spaces.

INTRODUCTION xvii

Drawing on drama to build connections among students, texts, and the world

The next three chapters reveal the myriad connections that are possible through drama. We begin with Carmen Medina's chapter, in which she explores common place locations and multiple sign systems. In her research with Latino/Latina students, she uncovers the ways students connected with themselves through literacy, literature, and drama. Further, her research makes visible how immigrant children used drama to navigate interpretive spaces that are informed by a convergence of historical, personal, and cultural meaning systems. The result is a detailed account of the ways these children related to and used literacy across languages, contexts, and borders. Next, Karen Kelley examines a classroom project in which students maintained the roles of literary characters (connecting with the text and self) while exploring issues within and around the novel *The Watsons Go to Birmingham— 1963*. These explorations required the students to grapple with ways to enter the worlds of "others" across cultures. Kelley explores the workings of a group of Caucasian/Latina girls who take on the role of Joetta, an African American. She describes their attempts to bring their character to the forefront in a novel filled with issues of racism, delinquency, and violence. Trisha Wies Long's chapter brings this section "full circle" with her examination of a process that allows students to read and interpret visual literacy, thereby engaging students in arts-based activism that connects them to the world. Using pictures of the segregated South, Wies Long describes how children can connect to injustices in the past and act on them in the present.

Creating critical stances with drama, texts, and society

In the last three chapters, the authors reveal the theoretical, practical, physical, and critical stances that students can take through drama. First, Jenifer Jasinski Schneider shares classroom examples of a teacher who used process drama as a site for negotiating freedom, voice, and choice with the students. The effects of student freedom are also examined through moments when the children learned to question themselves, their worlds, and even their teacher. Carmen Córdova presents a qualitative study in which children learned to care deeply for others and developed a sophisticated sense of morality through the exploration of literature through drama. In particular, she examines how her students' responses were reified through drama and how their imagination and engagement enabled them to develop seven sophisticated theories of moral reasoning. Finally, Beth Murray concludes the book with a chapter that summarizes where drama has been (in academic, artistic, and educational terms) and theorizes where drama might go. She explores how we prioritize our responsibility to and advocacy for drama as an art form and an educational tool for young people who are reflections of and participants in our complex, diverse society.

THE EDUCATIVE VALUE OF PROCESS DRAMA

We feel that this collection builds on O'Neill's ideas of bringing together process drama practices and aesthetics of theater as outlined in *Drama Worlds* (1995) and extends that link in two ways. First, authors in this collection question how process drama can help learners examine their own subjectivities—or their ideological and personal meaning systems— and reposition those subjectivities to take multiple perspectives within the communities of their classrooms (Harre & Langenhove 1999). Curriculum and drama researcher Kathleen Gallagher theorizes about the role of community to link educational drama and theater (Gallagher and Booth 2003). She argues for what she calls "theatre pedagogy," in which "we are—as players—to make manifest our own subjectivities in the world evoked through character and play" (13). Chapters in this volume evoke worlds and traverse real and imaginary communities to demonstrate how drama can help teachers and their students unpack their own meaning systems and ways of knowing.

For example, in her chapter on *full circling*, Trisha Wies Long writes, "as I walked solemnly around the room and tapped each child on the shoulder, some slowly and some quickly—a symphony of voices emerged" (Chapter 6). Wies Long explains that the children were able to use their voices as lenses to look more carefully at how identity shapes understanding of the civil rights movement. In addition, Carmen Medina theorizes about the ways in which immigrant children interactively read texts and themselves and explores how, through drama, children "begin to articulate multiple ways in which they perceive texts and self" (Chapter 4). Both of these chapters map practices onto theory and help reposition that theory within a context that illustrates a potential for process drama to create a space for students and teachers to think differently about literacy learning.

Second, the chapters in this volume redefine the nature of text by blurring the lines between the literary texts, the roles participants assume when involved in drama, and the audience for dramatic work. This redefinition aligns with what performance theorist Ric Knowles has described as "reading the material theatre" (2004), in which he argues for a multidimensional approach for analyzing dramatic performances that consider a text, the production, and reception of the event. These three aspects are mutually constitutive and shape the drama work in interesting and profound ways. For example, Kari-Lynn Winters, Theresa Rogers, and Andrew Schofield detail how reading and writing practices are transformed in drama based on the Greek tragedy *Antigone* (Chapter 3). In their account, the drama work framed and reframed the reading, writing, and meaning-making processes of students. They write, "In this project, we saw how students were drawing on their background knowledge and experiences, composing, decoding, visualizing, revising, and negotiating social relationships in the interfaces of drama, literacy, and multimedia." The students, whose stories the authors tell in their chapter, performed other texts differently as a result of the drama work that they engaged in during the Antigone Project.

In another example of the power of voice, Jenifer Jasinski Schneider describes her work in one teacher's classroom in which students used drama to perform texts that challenged the boundaries of teacher and student (Chapter 7). She writes, "The children portrayed characters and wrote as characters different from themselves. At times they were children, at other times they were adults. They were peacemakers and immigrants. They were Sondra's students, but they were also her peers. And this unique relationship created boundary disputes in the classroom." Schneider's chapter lays out some of the pedagogical risks involved with using process drama as a feature of children's writing instruction and explains how multiple roles can create unexpected turns. Yet she also demonstrates that the drama work facilitated the development of powerful multiple literacies in these same children.

There are other examples of the educative value of process drama in each of the chapters, making this book valuable on four levels. First, it situates process drama work within the changing field of literacy studies and demonstrates what process drama offers to recent conceptualizations of multiple literacies. Second, it provides practical examples of how process drama can work in a variety of contexts with diverse learners. Third, it challenges teachers who are considering process drama as an aspect of their literacy teaching to think deeply about its potential for transforming curriculum. And finally, it suggests new theoretical directions for researchers who are investigating process drama as part of shifting landscapes of literacy.

REFERENCES

Bateson, Gregory. 1955. "A Theory of Play and Fantasy." *Psychiatric Research Reports* 2: 39–52.

Bateson, Gregory. 1973. *Steps to Ecology of Mind*. London: Paladin Books.

Bolton, Gavin. 1998. *Acting in Classroom Drama: A Critical Analysis*. Portland, ME: Calendar Island Publishers.

Bruner, Jerome. 1986. *Actual Minds, Possible Worlds*. Cambridge, MA: Harvard University Press.

Bruner, Jerome. 1990. *Acts of Meaning*. Cambridge, MA: Harvard University Press.

Cope, Bill, & Mary Kalantzis, eds. 2000. *Multiliteracies: Literacy Learning and the Design of Social Futures*. New York: Routledge.

Courtney, Richard. 1995. *Drama and Feeling: An Aesthetic Theory*. Montreal: McGill-Queen's University Press.

Gallagher, Karen, and David Booth, eds. 2003. *How Theatre Educates: Convergences, and Counterpoints with Artists, Scholars, and Advocates*. Toronto: University of Toronto Press.

Harre, Rom, and Luk van Langenhove, eds. 1999. *Positioning Theory: Moral Contexts of Intentional Action*. Oxford: Blackwell Publishing.

Knowles, Richard. 2004. *Reading the Material Theatre*. Cambridge: Cambridge University Press.

The New London Group. 1996. "A Pedagogy of Multiliteracies: Designing Social Futures." *Harvard Educational Review* 66 (1): 60–93.

O'Neill, Cecily. 1995. *Drama Worlds: A Frame for Process Drama*. Portsmouth, NH: Heinemann.

O'Neill, Cecily, and Alan Lambert. 1983. *Drama Structures: A Practical Handbook for Teachers*. Portsmouth, NH: Heinemann.

Vygotsky, Lev. 1978. *Mind in Society: The Development of Higher Psychological Processes*. Cambridge, MA: MIT University Press.

Wagner, Betty Jane. 1998. *Educational Drama and Language Arts: What Research Shows*. Portsmouth, NH: Heinemann.

1

Educational Drama as Response to Literature: Possibilities for Young Learners

Thomas P. Crumpler

What is the relationship between drama and reading? This question informed a workshop in which two colleagues and I worked with a group of teachers to explore relationships among drama, reading, and the interpretation of texts. The workshop focused on drama in education, or process drama, as a way to help learners imagine possibilities, explore roles, rehearse and revise oral language, and use these experiences to expand interpretations of texts. The teachers were a diverse group of professionals who brought varying backgrounds, interests, and classroom experiences to this all-day workshop. By the end of the day, we had moved quickly through several different works of literature, talked about the possibilities of drama for promoting rich interpretations of texts, engaged the teachers in some preliminary drama work, and discussed plans and hopes we had for using drama in our classrooms.

Working with these teachers as readers in a dramatic context suggested the complex relationships among readers, texts, drama, and the nature of interpretation. Later, reflecting on the nature of drama and the practices of reading, the group suggested a set of questions that were useful for thinking further about these relationships: How do readers perform texts as they read? How are readers positioned by texts? Can the types of imaginative and in-role moves that readers make as part of drama enable them to reposition the text and themselves in relationship to a text? What types of new texts are created by these repositionings? Does drama promote *response to literature*?

Although drama educators, researchers in reading, and literary theorists have noted reading and drama relationships, no one has fully described this relationship in a way that could serve as a frame for response to literature. In this chapter I explore and describe this relationship by drawing on selected work in literary and feminist criticism, recent theoretical scholarship in the teaching of reading, and drama in education. From this review I develop a model of reading response that is dramatic in nature, argue for implications for interpretation of texts, and suggest directions for research.

READING, DRAMA, AND THE SHIFTING NATURE OF TEXTS AND READERS

Literary Criticism

Robert Scholes' *Textual Power: Literary Theory and the Teaching of English* (1985), is useful to begin considering relationships between drama and reading. In the introductory section, "Pretext," Scholes argues for a particular role of texts in teaching:

> Texts are places where power and weakness become visible and discussable, where learning and ignorance manifest themselves, where structures that enable and constrain our thoughts become palpable. (xi)

The tensions that Scholes suggests between power and weakness as well as learning and ignorance may best become visible when explored through the use of dramatic structures such as working in role, developing tableaux, or participating in other structures that are part of classroom drama (O'Neill and Lambert 1982). As learners employ these drama structures to interact with and explore texts, they may be able to shift both their relationships to a text and their understanding of it. Scholes also articulates a goal for helping students read efficiently and critically when he states:

> We must help our students come into their own powers of textualization. We must help them see that every poem, play, and story is

a text related to others, both verbal pre-texts and social sub-texts, and all manner of post-texts, including their own responses, whether in speech, writing, or action. (20)

Scholes' views place the reader as text-maker in the sense that comprehension and understanding of what is read involves creating or re-creating another text. This process of creating and interacting aligns with approaches positing a constructivist role for a reader (e.g., Rosenblatt 1978.) Further, Scholes' statement on the nature of reading, which emphasizes that "reading involves knowledge of two types of codes: generic and cultural" (1985, 26), indicates the value of negotiation and interpretation as central processes in reading. The generic codes are the grammar or structures of stories that readers use to aid in the comprehension of texts as they read. Cultural codes involve the explicit ways readers use their experiences with language to "construct a fictional world" (27). Scholes sees understanding these cultural codes as a semiotic process and central for reading, because it enables readers to locate themselves within and navigate through these constructed worlds. These processes of locating and navigating the worlds constructed by readers as they interact with texts can be better understood when conceptualized from a dramatic perspective.

The emphasis Scholes placed on reading as a constructive process in which readers draw on cultural knowledge to position themselves within fictional worlds is enriched in the recent work of Iser (1989). In an essay exploring relationships among reading, interpretation, and the concept of performance, Iser sought to establish a dynamic relationship between the text and the reader, viewing the interaction as a "performative act" (236–248). Iser describes it this way:

The text itself becomes a kind of junction, where other texts, norms, and values meet and work upon each other; as point of intersection its core is virtual, and only when actualized by the potential recipient—does it explode into its plurivocity. (238)

In Iser's view, making sense of a text involves "actualizing" it or performing its meaning. Additionally, intertextual processes, whereby previous texts and "norms and values" inform one another as a reader actualizes the present text, characterize this performance. Iser's norms and values resonate with Scholes' cultural codes, as both theorists conceptualize a key aspect of reading as negotiating understanding through and with cultural knowledge. Iser's notion of reading and interpretation of texts also includes another dramatic concept—staging. He draws an analogous relationship between an actor and reader as a way to explicate the aesthetic features of reading. Iser argues that to "produce the form of an indeterminate character, the actor must allow his own reality to fade out." Thus in Iser's view the actor is simultaneously himself and others as a text is performed. Similarly, "the reader finds himself in much the same situation" and "staging oneself as someone else is a source of aesthetic pleasure; it is also the means whereby representation is transferred from text to reader" (1989, 244). The terms *representation* and *staging* are useful for developing a dramatic model of reading, as they are recursively situated within the processes of reading. In other words, readers stage meaning by negotiating a text through cultural and structural codes and represent that meaning to themselves and others. Representation entails intertextual processes in which readers forge linkages with other *texts* (literary and cultural) as they comprehend.

For example, as I was reading Iser's chapter "Representation: A Performative Act" as part of the research for this article, I staged myself both purposively, as an academic selectively drawing upon the work of a literary theorist to construct a dramatic model of reading, and generally, as an admiring reader fascinated by the breadth of Iser's scholarship. Simultaneously I represented this text against other works I have read by this author (specifically, *The Act of Reading* and *The Implied Reader*) and other theoretical texts and studies in reader-response criticism. I considered how much I use the concept of response as part of the teaching I do now (i.e., requiring the graduate students I teach to respond to research articles) and recognized how reader response as a way to analyze/stage what we do as readers has become a rich way to think about literature. All of these intertextual links were folded into how I represented Iser's chapter in my mind and the attempts I make in this essay to make that representation visible. This reflection on my own reading process brings the concept of positionality—how readers are positioned by and position themselves in relation to a text—to the fore. Iser introduced this concept later in the same essay cited above as our "decentered position" (1989, 244), which he describes as the human need to step outside of ourselves to understand our own identity. However, the importance of positionality as it relates to reading is more fully explored in the recent feminist work of Lynne Pearce (1997).

Feminist Criticism

In her text *Feminism and the Politics of Reading* (1997), feminist cultural critic Lynn Pearce examines and critiques the practices of reading within a gendered context. Specifically, Pearce analyzes "the full emotional range of the reading process" (19) as a way to consider "how the reader-viewer gets involved with textual character . . . what happens once they have arrived there; how their 'identifications' change; how they mutate and perish" (18). Pearce's work is pertinent to a dramatic view of reading because she anchors her theory in Roland Barthes' emphasis on the pleasure involved in reading and interpreting texts (*S/Z* 1974; *The Pleasure of the Text* 1975) and then argues for a view of reading as "romance." In her view, the metaphor of reading as romance "requires that we identify exactly who, or what, aspect of the text/(con)textual experience the reader engages in her interaction with it" (Pearce 1997, 9). Further, Pearce suggests that critics who have explored the pleasure/emotional aspects of reading have focused narrowly on a male context, which has been limited to "the moment of recognition, identification, and perhaps interpretation and not on the emotional hinterland beyond." Finally, Pearce sought to examine her own reading processes and others to make visible a view of reading that turns on models of romance and desire that "go beyond the Freudian 'pleasure principle'" to provide space for a "fuller range of emotional experience" (11).

To do this Pearce draws on cultural and feminist scholarship to reconfigure the conception of reader as "spectator/viewer" (which she argues has been primarily described cognitively) to include "the textual other" (1997, 17). Pearce explains it this way:

> As I have also already indicated, the textual other can be represented by things as well as a character in the text: it might also take form of a "structure of feeling," an interlocutory subject position (how a character positions us), an author function, an interpretive community or the (covert/overt) audience/addressee of our own reading. (17)

In other words, this *positioning* and *repositioning* of oneself as a reader in relation to a textual other involves dynamic interactions of power between that text and how an individual reader makes meaning of it (Pearce 1997). More specifically, reader-text relationships may be passive, in which a text dominates a reader and the reader is positioned as a spectator. Alternatively, a reader may position himself or herself in a more interactive, critical stance, or a reader may negotiate some hybrid position—reading for multiple purposes and reflecting on how the construction of a textual other allows for a range of emotional interactions. For example, in her earlier work on feminism and reading, Pearce argues that reading the poetry of Dante Gabriel Rossetti as a feminist allows her to see Rossetti's work differently, and read *against* its tendency as text to *masculinize* a reader's experience (1997). Conceiving of reading in this way, as do Scholes and Iser, places intertextual processes at the center of meaning-making and implies that reading is a performative act that mobilizes multiple intertextual resources.

How does Pearce's work inform a dramatic view of reading then? The construction of a textual other that she claims as central to reading exists in a dialogue with our own consciousness of ourselves as readers. This idea resonates with Iser's concept of staging. For both critics, reading is a dramatic activity in which a reader stages his or her understanding of texts by imaginatively, emotionally, and intellectually interacting with them through intertextual processes. Returning to one of the questions framing this essay (Can the types of imaginative and in-role moves that readers make as part of drama enable them to reposition the text and themselves in relationship to a text?) helps clarify the usefulness of viewing reading from a dramatic frame. The answer to this question is yes, because the type of work entailed in physically engaging in process or educational drama (e.g., teacher-in-role, tableau, students-in-role, and so on) mirrors processes of reading as described in the theoretical work of Iser and Pearce in two ways. First, process drama, as Cecily O' Neill points out, "involves making, shaping, and appreciating a dramatic event, an experience that articulates experience" (1995, 1). Reading and interpreting texts also involves making, shaping, and appreciating, and those processes are refracted through intertextual others and staged as scenes of understanding by a reader. Through engagement in drama work that allows readers to interact and explore texts within a community of participants, the internal processes of a reader are recast as aspects of the drama making. Second, a key element of process drama involves exploring the emotional range of responses, which Pearce argues is central to a fuller understanding of reading processes. This exploration unfolds as participants/readers position and reposition their own and others' understandings of pre-texts, texts, and other artifacts that become part of the collaboratively constructed drama world (O'Neill 1995).

To complete this dramatic model of reading and attempt to answer the last two questions I posed—what types of new texts are created by these repositionings, and does drama promote response to reading—I draw on work from three recent texts in drama education: *Drama Worlds* (O'Neill 1995), *Acting in Classroom Drama: A Critical Analysis* (Bolton 1998), and *The Dramatic Arts and Cultural Studies: Acting Against the Grain* (Berry 2000). Following this discussion, a synthesis outlining features of this model of reading is articulated. Finally, directions for future research are explored.

LINKING PROCESS DRAMA AND READING

In the introduction to the book in which she argues for connecting process drama with structures of contemporary theater, O'Neill (1995) explains the problematic nature of analyzing theatrical performances:

> Attempts to analyze any theater event, however detailed, can never be more than tentative and partial. It is impossible to reconstruct the totality of any performance, but it is possible to grasp some of its organizing principles; and the same is true of even an essentially improvised event like process drama. (xix)

Analyzing a reading event has essentially the same challenges. It is impossible to reconstruct the totality of a reader's encounter with a text. Researchers and theorists are able to grasp and describe some of the organizing principles, such as the notions that readers draw on multiple meaning systems, use contextual resources, develop intertextual practices, and make sense of texts through cultural and ideological frames. However, the event of reading is always/already more than these principles. It is the role of the reader in the making/performing of his or her own understanding of texts that continues to be elusive to researchers in literacy. One of the major shifts in research into literacy in the last 25 years has been a focus on the role of the reader in processes of comprehension (Tierney 1994). Researchers have examined reading or literacy behaviors through analyzing language processes, patterns of miscues, studies of readers responding to texts, and inquiring into sociocultural processes that inform and shape the ways readers comprehend texts (e.g., Halliday 1994; Goodman and Goodman 1994; Squire 1994; Moll 1994). These studies and others heighten the role of a reader in the reading process. In his most recent work, Gavin Bolton undertakes an analogous task by historically and theoretically analyzing acting behaviors in classroom drama and then developing a conceptual framework that synthesizes a "common ground of all acting behaviors" (1998, 250). Bolton offers the following:

> Acting behavior is an act of fiction making involving identification through action, a prioritizing of determining responsibilities, the conscious manipulation of time and space and a capacity for generalization. It relies on some sense of audience, including self-spectatorship. (270)

Significant for conceptualizing a dramatic model of reading is the individual agency implicit in his definition. As participants in drama events are involved in "fiction making," so too are readers involved in meaning making as they interact with texts. The same process of identification with character, prioritizing information, a manipulation of time and space, generalizing and revising understanding, and self-spectatorship are features of reading. Coupled with the notion that the totality of any reading event can only be partially analyzed, the role of the reader/actor as central to meaning/fiction making is significant on two levels. First, dramatic repositioning within and against texts as part of reading becomes more understandable. As a reader interacts with a text, she or he may be positioned as an individual being assessed or tested, a person assigned to read for information, and other positions defined by a teacher or other outside authority. Further, the text itself may position the reader as a spectator/viewer of events within a narrative sequence. And additionally, the reader may position himself/herself as suspect of the truthfulness of a text, an advocate for a particular character, and other possibilities arising within the comprehension process.

Within a dramatic model of reading, the assuming of multiple roles or positions in relationship to a text is viewed as a key feature of the reading process. Teachers would consciously structure instructional opportunities for readers to take up roles and reposition themselves within or against texts through work in role, tableau, dialogue writing, games that build community, and other dramatic structures. These would lead readers to pursue/improvise other unexpected positions as they became involved in fiction/meaning making. In this way, the internal drama of readers making sense of texts could be aligned with class instructional practices. Second, new types of texts are created in the process and as a result of repositioning through drama work. For example, in a class of first graders, I read Maurice Sendak's *Where the Wild Things Are*. Prior to reading the story, we previewed the text by looking at the pictures and talking about what a wild thing might be like. Then, as a group, we made sounds a wild thing might make.

During the story, we stopped and talked about the main character, Max, and whether he was really going to the island or just dreaming, and what they thought of Max's relationship with his mother and where the father might be in the story. This very preliminary dramatic work of asking who is not in the story (thus creating space for other characters and other relationships) allowed the first-grade students to read the text in more imaginative ways. One result was that the girls began imagining Max's sister (whom they named Maxina) and speculating how she might fit into the story. Later in our drama work together the children traveled back to the island, with the boys in role as Max and the girls in role as Maxina. It seemed that the drama work we did in a sense served as a catalyst so that as a result of repositioning, a new *text* was created. This new text had an additional character that was read into the story, shifting the action in a specific way. By drawing on a dramatic conception of reading, the children were able to become more active makers/performers of their own interactions with a text.

The ability to read critically is (in addition to making and performing) a salient feature of reading. In the book in which she argues for linking the dramatic arts and cultural studies, Kathleen Berry emphasizes that to read critically means to examine how we are positioned as subjects/objects by the discourses of contemporary culture (2000). Further, she believes that viewing the dramatic arts through theories informing cultural studies helps us to see new possibilities for drama. As she puts it:

> Through the agency of dramatic arts informed by cultural studies and criticism, we can consider the crisis of modern life and rehearse possible re-imaginings. (6)

The crisis that Berry refers to is a crisis whose meanings are valued and heard in a postmodern culture. In other words,

> certain knowledge, truths, race, age, sexuality, subjectivity, authorship, borders, values, histories, and a host of other constructions are all problematic. We are positioned and how we are positioned adds to the difficulty of entering the world, re-visioning it as inclusive of all knowledge, truth subjectivities, and other earlier-mentioned constructions. (2000, 7)

How we are positioned also may impact the difficulty readers have in entering texts. In addition, developing a dramatic model of reading suggests how we might construct other ways to help readers interact with texts and become more conscious of how they are making/performing their own understanding of texts. Berry's work is important to this dramatic model of reading because it suggests that ideological issues are at work in reading processes. Developing a more fully articulated model of a dramatic conception of reading could help teachers reimagine reading instruction and researchers consider new ways to inquire into literacy practices. It is this model that I now outline.

TOWARD A DRAMATIC MODEL OF RESPONSE TO LITERATURE

Based on the scholarship cited above, the dramatic model of response to literature I am arguing for has the following features:

- Response to literature is a meaning making/performative act involving intertextual processing on multiple levels simultaneously.
- A feature of these intertextual processes is constructing a relationship with a "textual other" that allows readers to explore/dramatize a broad range of emotional responses to texts.
- This dramatization enacts a relationship that can be characterized as a "romance" or similar interactive relationship in which readers stage their own understanding of texts within networks of intellectual and emotional response.
- The dramatic process of response to literature cannot be reduced to a collection of discrete parts as the reader/actor's experience is more than a collection of parts because the process itself is informed by multiple systems of meaning.
- As readers are positioned by texts, understanding reading from a dramatic perspective will aid readers in repositioning themselves within and against texts as they perform response to and interpretation of literary texts.
- Because reading involves negotiating ideological and cultural discourses, a dramatic model of reading provides structures that help readers question, critique, and evaluate the texts they are interacting with in terms of the dynamics of power.

This emergent dramatic model of response has implications for the way teachers plan and implement reading instruction that includes response to literature as an important component. A few examples will illustrate possibilities. At the phonemic level, teachers may want to engage readers more frequently in activities that allow them to perform sound/letter relationships both as themselves and in role with other children as part of process drama work. This would activate multiple meaning systems and involve what has been called the "whole being of the learner" (Crumpler and Schneider 2002, 78). At the word and syntactic level, teachers could have children develop tableaux as part of drama work in which they explore representing the texture, shape, or nature of words and sentences as a feature of reading instruction. This approach would encourage children to dramatize both the concrete realities and subtle nuances of words and sentences. On the semantic/discourse level, teachers could engage children in entering texts in multiple ways—such as talking to a character, asking who is not in the story, whose story it is, who acts and who is acted upon, who speaks and who is silenced, what is valued and how value is determined—and from these and other questions develop drama sequences that take readers into the text and beyond, where they have opportunities to imagine and explore possibilities of meaning.

These are a few possibilities, and there are many others. One important point to note is that while I recognize the importance of development in learning, I do not believe that engaging the dramatic processes of reading at the semantic/discourse level must be delayed until children are older. My experience is that kindergarten, first-, and second-grade learners are capable of negotiating complex and multifaceted readings of texts (Crumpler and Schneider 2002).

What are the implications for research engendered by this model? Researchers who are interested in inquiring into the nature of reading and literacy from a dramatic frame could begin to explore two levels of questions. One area of interest would be to examine the relationships between the internal dramatic processes of readers and the instructional practices in drama work in terms of how the dramatic and interpretive moves that participants make in sequences of process drama affect the internal processes of individual readers. Might there be a progressive refinement of dramatic meaning-making strategies as readers become in tune metacognitively with their own thinking, feeling, and doing with texts? A second area of interest has to do more with issues of reading critically and critiquing ideological issues in texts. If reading is a dramatic process, how does drama work enable a reader to more effectively look at the ways texts position them? Can we use a dramatic model to help readers more actively question the structures of their own cultures in Freire and Macedo's sense of "reading the world" (1987, 35)? Further, if readers were able to reposition themselves through understanding reading dramatically, would this help them draw on background knowledge in more diverse ways? These and other questions could lead researchers to develop more complete understandings of how readers are actively performing their understandings of texts and provide richer ways to help readers rehearse and stage those understandings.

CONCLUSION: THE DRAMATIC VALUE OF IMAGINATION AND THE FICTIONAL

In his book on the nature of fiction, Pavel (1986) argued that a new theory of fiction can "respond again to the world creating powers of the imagination" and help us see how fictional texts configure into the "general economy of culture" (10). An aspect of Pavel's theory is the value of refocusing our attention on the power of imagination to enter into fictional worlds created in the tension of the *what is* and the *what if* that informs the reading of literary works. He argues against too much reliance on what he calls "the constraints of the textual approach," or an overreliance on the language of literature to convey meaning.

I would argue for a similar role for a dramatic model of response to literature. Teachers, aware of the potential *intertextuality and romance* of reading literature (both cognitive and emotional) outlined in the model, can help learners respond to literature through drama in deep, richer ways. These responses could free students to perform understandings of what they read and use educational drama to explore complex issues across multiple domains and then critique those understandings through the use of the multiple lenses that educational drama offers. American schools are struggling to balance testing and accountability against a need to help young learners to read texts that are increasingly multimodal and a hybrid of the real and the fictional. Drama as response to literature becomes as important as any work we do in classrooms. It allows teachers and students to begin to read, critique, and evaluate those texts in ways that enhance understanding of how texts work, release them from the constraints of a single "correct" interpretation, and allow them to gain insights into their own literacy learning processes.

REFERENCES

Barthes, Roland. 1974. *S/Z*. Trans. Richard Miller. New York: Hill and Wang.

Barthes, Roland. 1975. *The Pleasure of the Text*. Trans. Richard Miller. New York: Hill and Wang.

Berry, Kathleen. 2000. *The Dramatic Arts and Cultural Studies: Acting Against the Grain*. New York: Falmer Press.

Bolton, Gavin. 1998. *Acting in Classroom Drama: A Critical Analysis*. Staffordshire, England: Trentham Books Limited.

Crumpler, Thomas, and Jenifer Jasinski Schneider. 2002. "Writing with Their Whole Being: A Cross Study Analysis of Children's Writing from Five Classrooms Using Process Drama." *Research in Drama Education*, 7 (1): 61–79.

Freire, Paulo, and Donaldo Macedo. 1987. *Literacy: Reading the Word and the World*. South Hadley, MA: Bergin & Garvey Publishers.

Goodman, Ken, and Yetta Goodman. 1994. "To Err Is Human: Learning About Language Processes by Analyzing Miscues." In *Theoretical Models and Processes of Reading*, 4th ed., edited by R. Ruddell, M. Ruddell, and H. Singer, 104–123. Newark, DE: International Reading Association.

Halliday, Michael. 1994. "The Place of Dialogue in Children's Construction of Meaning." In *Theoretical Models and Processes of Reading*, 4th ed., edited by R. Ruddell, M. Ruddell, and H. Singer, 70–82. Newark, DE: International Reading Association.

Iser, Wolfgang. 1989. *Prospecting: From Reader Response to Literary Anthropology*. Baltimore: Johns Hopkins University Press.

Moll, Luis. 1994. "Literacy Research in Communities and Classrooms: A Sociocultural Approach." In *Theoretical Models and Processes of Reading*, 4th ed., edited by R. Ruddell, M. Ruddell, and H. Singer, 179–206. Newark, DE: International Reading Association.

O'Neill, Cecily. 1995. *Drama Worlds: A Framework for Process Drama*. Portsmouth, NH: Heinemann.

O'Neill, Cecily, and Alan Lambert. 1982. *Drama Structures: A Practical Handbook for Teachers*. London: Hutchinson.

Pavel, Thomas. 1986. *Fictional Worlds*. Cambridge, MA: Harvard University Press.

Pearce, Lynn. 1997. *Feminism and the Politics of Reading*. London: Arnold.

Rosenblatt, Louis. 1978. *The Reader, the Text, the Poem*. Carbondale, IL: Southern Illinois University Press.

Scholes, Robert. 1985. *Textual Power: Literary Theory and the Teaching of English*. New Haven, CT: Yale University Press.

Squire, James. 1994. "Research in Reader Response, Naturally Interdisciplinary." In *Theoretical Models and Processes of Reading*, 4th ed., edited by R. Ruddell, M. Ruddell, and H. Singer, 637–652. Newark, DE: International Reading Association.

Tierney, Robert. 1994. "Dissensions, Tensions, and the Models of Literacy." In *Theoretical Models and Processes of Reading*, 4th ed., edited by R. Ruddell, M. Ruddell, and H. Singer, 1162–1182. Newark, DE: International Reading Association.

2

Story Drama Structures: Building Supports for Multiple Literacies

Juliana Saxton and Carole Miller

> Story dramas make possible ways of engaging deeply, richly with texts that are not dependent on decoding, that don't require being able *independently* to read words. While the text is the focus and understanding it certainly the point, the techniques for accessing that text are multi-modal, experiential, participatory and forgivingly open-ended. (Preece 2004)

Drama engages students in a particular mode of learning that is experiential and social. In this chapter, we present a story drama structure that will serve as a practical demonstration of how drama supports multiple literacies, while at the same time offering opportunities for the social (or "hidden") curriculum. When students engage holistically with the meanings offered in the story, they develop new understanding of the content at both the interpersonal and the intrapersonal levels (Gardner 1983). They do so by exploring human behaviours and experiences in social circumstances under fictional pressure. Process drama educates through "knowledge in," through a multiplicity of metalanguages; it requires that each student bring his/her own personal contexts and feelings into play, for they are the fabric with which the fictional world is woven.

In 1967, the Plowden Report on schools in the United Kingdom noted that "what is most remarkable now in many infant [primary] schools is the variety of writing: writing rising out of dramatic play" (218). John Stewig, in *Spontaneous Drama: A Language Art* (1973) pointed out that speaking and listening were other ways of writing and reading. Since then, literacy has become an ever more expanded collective noun that addresses the multiple ways in which we are/can become/must become literate.

To be literate, in our terms, is to be able to function in the world as a participant in, contributor to, and shaper of a democratic society. We offer this qualifier because it places us and our students within a society that makes certain demands upon and requires certain skills from its citizens. In *The Unconscious Civilization*, John Ralston Saul writes that a "citizen-based democracy is built upon (disinterested) participation" (1995, 35). Becoming the kind of citizen Saul is talking about requires people who have a clear understanding of themselves and of their intentionalities and the ability to see those in relation to the good of the whole. Participation requires more than an understanding of self; it includes being alive to others and the ability to exercise not just sympathy, but that much more difficult (difficult because it is active, rather than passive) quality of empathy. Empathy, or the placing of ourselves in others' shoes, lets us know from our own experience what an "other" could be feeling and thinking, and it is, as the novelist Ian McEwan reminds us (2001), an essential characteristic of what it means to be human. Participation requires the ability to communicate, the strength to take risks, and a tolerance for ambiguities (Barron 1988) and, as we are all aware, learning *about* is different from learning *through* participation.

On a more local level, Nigel Hall (1998) draws our attention to the dichotomy between the use of literacy in schools and the use of literacy outside school. Literacy in schools, he writes, is often "treated as an autonomous object, one that has a life-world of its own, unconnected to the ways in which it is actually used by people in their lives" (9). In describing work with young children in a drama context, he cites the "*real-worldness* of sociodramatic play" (Hall's italics) in which drama affords authentic, challenging, and engaging contexts. During a twelve-week period, the children work through a situation in which they really care about the outcomes. As they engage in more than twenty literacy activities that demand they deal with a number of complex issues, Hall notes the reciprocal nature of literacy activities and drama. Writing a letter of persuasion (for example) would have no meaning without the dramatic context that provides the impetus to negotiate. Rather than seeing literacy practices as "independent and neutral competencies" unconnected to their lives outside school (Street and Street 1991, 150), students use their literacy skills in situations that demand their participation. It is, Hawkins writes, the kind of "apprenticeship into the very specific forms of [social] languages and literacies represented inside and outside the classroom" (2004, 17) that makes drama such a rich pedagogy. As a significant curriculum integrator for the teaching of literacies, O'Mara (2003) notes that drama is already affecting the primary and secondary curricula guides in the UK.

For the past six years, we have been piloting story drama structures that are built around children's picture books. While the work is designed for elementary and middle school students, we have found that when we introduce the structures, teachers and preservice teachers are as enthusiastic about entering the story as are their students. Our aim is that the structures will act as "scaffolds" to provide clear, thorough guidelines (tested with success in classrooms) upon which teachers can build their drama practice. These structures act as "occasions of conspiracy" (Barone 1990) in which all the players, teachers included, explore a "reality that resides neither in the literary work as object-in-the-world nor in the subjective 'mind' . . . but within a continuous experience between the two" (306). This "metaxis" (Boal 1995)—the ability to hold both worlds in the mind at the same time and to flicker between the two as the drama unfolds—is what enables the drama to be consciously experienced. Engaging aesthetically with the content, Barone continues, opens up "multiplicities of experience, conditions it, plants it specifically in virtual space and time . . ." (309). It is this "planting" that makes the reflective activities possible and they, in turn, are key to seeding further learning.

R. K. Sawyer (2004) details his concerns with "contemporary reform efforts towards scripted instruction that denies the creativity of teachers" (12). Indeed, the design of the structures appears, at first glance, to be similar to a teaching script. What is different, however, is that there is no script of students' responses, although we may suggest (rarely) one or two as examples to clarify an activity. In our experience, the teacher's "script" is what encourages generalist teachers to "have a go at doing some drama." Those teachers with experience simply use the structures as starting points for their own explorations into the stories. For novice *drama* teachers, the story drama structures act initially as a safety net; as they develop experience and come to know their classes, these teachers begin to create their own story drama structures.

In any case, Sawyer goes on to say, "there must be some structure to the classroom . . . even flexible, creative teachers . . . have plans and goals for each lesson." What the story drama structures do is to provide ways, as he puts it, to "conceptualize creative teaching within curricular structures through which teachers are able to develop improvised classroom discourse" (16). It is this discourse, stimulated by open-ended questions and attention to reflection, that is both the reward of teaching and, for those less experienced, the challenge.

Constructivist teaching methods are used by many teachers as a means of "making school more 'fun'" and, more often than not, the active learning techniques they are using are "frequently disconnected from actual learning" (Schutz 2004, 18). This is certainly true for the teachers and administrators who often view drama education in that light. They have difficulty understanding that drama education is more than putting on plays and is not just about providing some "fun" activities as a change of pace from the *real* curriculum. Those of us who recognize the power of drama as a means of enhancing learning have always to consider how we can inform others or, rather, find ways to help them to listen. But when these structures (or indeed, any process dramas) are read through the lens of literacy development, educators see that they are frameworks for effective literacy instruction (O'Mara 2003). The frameworks organize an array of instructional strategies and techniques that construct learning environments to provide experiences that generate new meanings and understandings from a multiplicity of viewpoints and standpoints: teachers', students', society's, and the culture's.

The traditional approach to using story as a resource for drama is exemplified by the work of the early American drama educator Winifred Ward. The story is re-enacted as each piece of the plot is played out sequentially. For example, in *Cinderella*, the story begins with Cinderella scrubbing the hearth and ends with the wedding. Roles are cast, scenes are delineated, and the language, while improvised, follows the story closely. In more current practice, we might start by entering into the middle of the story, showing the students a shoe that was found in a garden. Where did it come from? What kind of person could it belong to? Who might we ask? We could begin before the story by planning the menu for a ball. What sorts of food and drink would be appropriate for a young man's introduction to society? Exploring the themes and context for the story might lead us to ask, "I wonder what might cause someone to treat another badly?" If the story is read aloud as the starting point, we could move into drama by asking such questions as, "If you were the Prince, what would you say to your future sisters-in-law? How might you include them in the celebrations?" We could go beyond the story by asking, "As the stepsisters, you note that the wedding is two weeks away and you haven't yet received your invitations. To whom might you write about this glaring omission?" And because process drama is not necessarily sequential, any of these suggestions could become starting, middle, or end points, or provide reflection in and out of role. We are not confined to the story line; the structures allow teachers and students to see that the events in the story are only a part of the story and that we can play "on the line of the story, between the lines or beyond the lines" (Brownlie, Close, and Wingren 1988; Manzo 1969). In drama, we are always looking to find what lies beneath the lines (the subtext).

We are presently piloting a new story drama structure that provides examples of multiple literacies in action. We use the same framework for this story drama structure as we do for those found in *Into the Story: Language in Action Through Drama* (Miller and Saxton 2004a). For this chapter, we also suggest some analyses of the multiple literacies embedded in the first five activities; you may, of course, see others.

"—AND QUICK AS THAT—"
Based on *The Follower*
Written by Richard Thompson and illustrated
by Martin Springett

Why Did We Choose This Story?
- It is particularly appropriate for fall and winter seasons because the text captures the sense of weather.
- Like *The House that Jack Built*, in this cumulative story the language is strongly patterned and full of imagery, as are the illustrations.
- Central to the story and to each illustration is a mystery. Who is the woman, where does she go, why does she go there, and who follows her?

Key Understandings and Questions
- Being needed is fundamental to a well-balanced existence.
- What is it an animal companion can offer that is special?
- How do the tensions between the elements of theatre (sound/silence, movement/stillness, light/dark) enhance our understanding of the text?

1. Preparing to enter the story_____ 5 minutes

Grouping: Whole class in a circle
Strategy: Movement
Administration: Tambourine
Focus: Exploring space and pace

TEACHER: Before we begin our drama, we are going to warm up our bodies, as well as our imaginations. You will have to concentrate really hard to remember who you are. As I go around the circle, I will give each of you a letter: A, B, or C. Listen carefully so that you can remember.
A's, raise your hands, B's, raise your hands, C's, raise your hands.

It is useful to check with the students before beginning the activity.

TEACHER: When I give the signal, A's, you are to move *quickly* around the room, B's move at a *normal* pace, C's move *very slowly*. Be very careful not to bump into anyone. Keep good spaces between each other.
When you hear the tambourine, stop. Listen to the next instruction. Ready? Off you go.

After a few moments, sound the tambourine.

CHANGE. This time B's move *very slowly*, C's move *quickly*, and A's move at a *normal* pace.

As above.

TEACHER: Now, the last time: C's move at a *normal* pace, B's move *quickly*, and A's move *very slowly*.
And freeze. Please sit down where you are.
Choose one of those speeds and think about what it brought into your mind; what situations were you reminded of? Talk with the people next to you. [They talk]
Who heard something they would like to share with the group? [Hear]

Analysis

Type of Literacy Kinaesthetic understanding of the self in space and in relation to others

Description When we embody language, we ask the students to interpret words physically. Language in the head or in the mouth is different from interpreting language in and through the body.

Application "Reading" embodied language involves students in making comparisons, modeling for one another, and adjusting their movements as changes happen.

Physical engagement mediates affective and cognitive understandings and deepens students' understanding of who they are in relation to others. The ability to read the signs of physical language is imperative to effective social communication.

2. Into the story_____10 minutes

Grouping: Whole class
Strategy: Reading a picture
Administration: Overhead projector (OHP); Overhead of the illustration of Thursday's storm
Focus: To mine the illustration for the details of the story

TEACHER: Now, let's move into our story. Make sure you can see the screen clearly. [They shift]
Look at this picture. [up on OHP]
What do you see? Where do you see that?

It is important for the students to be able to justify their observations.

TEACHER: What do you hear? Where do you see that?
How does the movement we have just done connect to this picture? [Hear]
How many of you have been in weather like this? [They raise hands].
Tell your partner about that experience. [They do]
Has anyone anything they would like to share?

Analysis
Type of Literacy
Visual literacy

Description Reading nonverbal signs from an image allows us to experience how messages are codified in visual form and how mood is conveyed. The students are not story-making (creating narratives is often their initial tendency). The emphasis is on what is seen or heard so that they learn to read signs *before* making assumptions; when assumptions or predictions *are* made, they are grounded.

Application Recognizing that each of us may see things differently, depending on our experiences and our position of viewing, is necessary for clear communication. Some of us see holistically, some of us see details, some of us see things we never realized were there! Drama is all about making the invisible visible.

3. Sounds of the storm_____7 minutes

Grouping: Whole group as above
Strategy: Soundscape
Administration: Picture as in Activity 2; chalkboard and chalk or chart paper and pen
Focus: To give a sense of reality to the wind

TEACHER: Let's see if we can make the picture come alive through sound. What sorts of sounds might we hear? Look carefully at the picture again; what possibilities for sound are in this picture?

As students offer, words are recorded.

TEACHER: Let's try to turn these words into their sounds. Let's start at the top of our list. Anyone who feels that they can make that word or those words come alive as sound, on the count of three, just go for it! [They do]
I wonder how we could orchestrate those sounds to make the story of the weathery day? In drama, we call this a "Soundscape."
What sounds shall we begin with? What will we layer in and how will we end it? [They suggest]

List the order on the board for a guide.

TEACHER: Let's try it and see how it sounds. [They experiment]
Who has a suggestion to make our Soundscape more weathery? [Hear suggestions]

If there is time, students may like to do the Soundscape more than once.

Analysis
Type of Literacy
  Auditory literacy
  Description Through the activity, we are given opportunities to translate images into the words for the sounds we imagine we hear; then, to interpret those words into their sounds. In sequencing the sounds, we create another kind of "picture" called a Soundscape.

  Application Silent reading requires the ability to imagine the "score." The ability to put the voice to the character on the page is a skill that is essential for proficient readers. Benton (1979) has characterized a reader not just as an interpreter but as a performer who builds a mental stage and fills it with people, scenes, and events from the text. Students who respond to literature by creating a drama transform the classroom into this "mental stage." Like playwrights, they create an alternate reality but, in this case, one that is shaped and generated by the "text" of the image (68–85).

4. Bringing the picture alive_____7 minutes
Grouping: Whole class as above; individual movement
Strategy: Movement, tableau, titling
Administration: Illustration as in Activity 2; tape or CD of Vaughn Williams' Symphony No. 7 (*Sinfonia antartica*), cut number 3 ("Landscape"); tambourine
Focus: To find ways of moving that create a sense of the illustration

TEACHER: Now, what about the movement that is here in this picture? Look carefully. Apart from the woman, what else is moving in the picture? [They identify]

These words may be listed on board.

TEACHER: Find your own space in the room. Close your eyes.
  In a moment, we are going to make the picture come alive through movement, but first, let's hear some music that might help us with our movement as we create a certain mood—a certain feeling—that we see in the picture. [They hear music for 30 seconds to a minute]

Now, as you listen to the music, choose to be one of the things that were moving in the picture. [Music on]

Teacher speaks over the music.

TEACHER: Let the music help your body find that shape and movement of the thing you have chosen. Experiment moving as that shape as you listen to the music. Keep your eyes closed while you do this. [They do for about a minute]
Relax for a moment.
We'll do it again, but this time when you hear the tambourine, you will freeze in whatever shape your body is in at that moment. [They work for 30 seconds to the music and freeze to the tambourine]
Without shifting your bodies and using only your peripheral vision, look around you. [They do]
As you look around, think about what might we title our frozen picture—our tableau. The words have to match what we see.
Good. Relax. Let's have your ideas. [They share titles]

5. Putting it all together _____ 5 minutes

Grouping: Whole class divided into 2 groups
Strategy: Soundscape and movement
Administration: Music as in Activity 4; tambourine for control if needed; dark cloak or raincoat with hood; walking stick
Focus: To add a new element to what is already known; to improvise responses

TEACHER: Now, we are going to form two groups.

Teacher divides the class in half.

One group will re-create the Soundscape and the other will re-create the movement.
Who would be willing to lead our orchestra—to be the conductor?

There may be more than one conductor because what is about to happen can be done more than once.

TEACHER: Where will our orchestra be? [They decide]

Before we begin, let's add to our picture. Is there someone who is prepared to take the role of the woman in the picture? She will be moving through our landscape.

If a number of students volunteer, choose one and suggest that we can do this more than once.

TEACHER: Where is the road that the woman will walk upon? [They decide]
Where will she begin and where will she stop? [They decide]
Decide where you need to be in order to create this moving picture. [They find their positions]

After the stage has been "set," offer the following.

TEACHER: I wonder if this cloak (and stick) will help us to believe that this is the woman in the story?
Are we ready?
Let's begin with the Soundscape to set the mood. And when those of you who are creating the environment feel it is right, begin your movement.
Woman, when the environment is established, begin your journey along the road.
Let's try it. Conductor, whenever you are ready. [They do]

After the first time through:

TEACHER: Just talk to the person next to you about that.
Has anyone any comments? [Hear]
If we were to do it again, what could we suggest that would help us to believe that it is real? [They make suggestions]

Based on students' responses, this scene can be replayed any number of times, using a different "woman" and switching the orchestra and the environment groups; each experience will feed the new role/s.

Analysis of Activities Four and Five

Type of Literacy Combining kinaesthetic, visual, and oral literacies and layering in a role to concretize students' individual "mental stages" (Benton 1979).

Description To integrate those mental stages into a collective vision (Brook 1987) where we share in the creation of meanings we are making.

Application How we transform objects or ourselves into other objects, roles, situations, or events through physical and verbal actions in pretend activities are, for Jerome Bruner (1983) one of the important ways in which we develop engaged and effective readers.

Note: *If the story drama structure is to take more than one lesson, this is a good place to break. For the new lesson, the game of "Grandmother's Footsteps" will provide preparation for the improvised activity, and serve as a way to refocus the students on the drama.*

6. Introducing the story_____ 5 minutes
Grouping: Whole class
Strategy: Reading aloud
Administration: The storybook
Focus: To bring students' pre-story experiences to the listening of the story.

TEACHER: Find a place where you can see the pictures. [They do]

Teacher reads the whole story of The Follower, *sharing the illustrations.*

7. Using the story for improvisation_____10 minutes
Grouping: Pairs
Strategy: Shadowing
Administration: Chart paper; pen; music (as in Activity 4)
Focus: To recall events in the story; to explore improvising in movement and with words

TEACHER: Who can remember some of the things the woman did to try to get rid of the cat? [Write up on chart paper]
Find a partner and a place in the room where you can work together without disturbing others.
Choose who will be A and who will be B.
A's, we are going to imagine that we are the woman.

B's, we are going to imagine that we are the shadowy cat following the woman.
Set yourselves up as the woman and the cat, ready to begin with the music.
When you hear the tambourine, A's, turn to see if something is following you.
Let's remember some of the things the woman said or did to the cat. [They suggest]
B's, your task is to stop *so still* that when the woman you are following turns back to you, she won't see you moving, however quickly she turns.
A's, you may want to add what the woman did or said as you turn.

Music on and freeze at the sound of the tambourine five or six times.

TEACHER: Talk to your partner about that. What made it real for you both?
Everyone, switch roles with your partner and do it again. But when you hear the tambourine for the last time—and I will say, "Last time"—the woman will turn and invite the cat to come in.
Anyone remember the words she said? [They suggest]
Good. You may use those words but if you can't remember them, use whatever words seem right for you.
Ready? Begin. [They do]

Music on and freeze two or three times before saying,

TEACHER: Last time. [They improvise the invitation]
Well done. How was it different this last time? [They share]

8. Extending the story_____ 7 minutes
Grouping: Whole class working individually
Strategy: Writing in role; selecting the best reason (synthesizing); memorizing
Administration: Paper and pencils
Focus: To reflect inside the story

TEACHER: Find your own private place and listen carefully as I pass out paper and pencils to everyone.

Speaking as the materials are passed out,

STORY DRAMA STRUCTURES

TEACHER: Imagine you are the woman. Your friend lives very far away and has no idea that you have adopted a cat.
Write to your friend, telling what it was that made you decide (after all that time rejecting it) that you would take this cat into your house. What is it about this cat that made you change your mind?
Begin writing and don't worry about spelling or punctuation; just explain your decision to your friend. [They write]

It is important not to rush through this strategy. Don't worry if students stop writing. You can say quietly, "I can see that some people are thinking very deeply about what they are writing." When most students appear to have finished,

TEACHER: *Stop now and reread your letter.*
Underline the sentence that best explains your reason for keeping the cat. Commit that reason to memory. [They do]

9. Discovering the reasons behind the ending of the story_____5 minutes

Grouping: Whole class working individually
Strategy: Tapping in
Administration: Students' written work
Focus: To concretize thinking and feeling; to justify a decision

TEACHER: In a moment, we are going to hear those reasons. I will come around and put my hand on your shoulder. When you feel my hand on your shoulder, we will hear why you have decided to keep the cat. In order to hear better, let's put on our cat's ears and listen for the reason that makes us feel most wanted.

Move around the room, placing your hand firmly on each student's shoulder. Leave your hand there until the student stops speaking. After each one has contributed,

TEACHER: Thank you. There were some excellent reasons for keeping the cat. Just turn to the person next to you and talk about what you heard and which reason or reasons you think would make a cat feel wanted.

If you conclude here, you will want to reflect on the whole process. Notice how these questions begin to unpack the Key Understandings and Questions.

If you decide on using further strategies (see below), you will want to return to these questions to help you and your students reflect on their work and on the story.

TEACHER: I wonder why this cat chose this particular woman. Many people must have walked along that road; why *this* woman?
A lot of us have pets. I wonder what is it about a pet that makes us want to keep it?
In drama, we talk about "going into" the story. How did the work we did with "Thursday's picture" prepare us to enter the story?

Other strategies that lead to further literacy activities:

Teacher in role

Why would I want a cat? What's a cat good for?

Or

I've never had a cat before. I am hoping that you can tell me how to look after one.

Brainstorming

What are suitable names for a cat? Which name(s) would be appropriate for this cat?

Writing an instructional pamphlet

How to make your cat feel at home.

Message writing

What might have been a message that caused the woman to make one of these journeys?

Imagining a life

Where might the woman be going?

What, or who, calls her out and why, I wonder?
Who looks after her child?

Thinking from the cat's point of view

What might the cat do to help the woman?

Making questions

What sorts of questions would we like to ask the woman? [Teacher then goes into role (using the cloak?) and responds to their questions]

Reference

Thompson, Richard (2000). *The Follower*. Markham, ON: Fitzhenry & Whiteside.

Materials needed:

Activity 1: Tambourine
Activity 2: OHP and overhead of illustration (Thursday's storm)
Activity 3: Illustration as in Activity 2; chalkboard and chalk or chart paper and pens
Activity 4: Illustration as in Activity 2; tape or CD of Symphony No. 7 (*Sinfonia antarctica*), cut number 3 ("Landscape"); tambourine
Activity 5: Music as in Activity 4; tambourine; cloak or dark raincoat with hood; walking stick
Activity 6: The storybook
Activity 7: Chart paper, pen; music as in Activity 4
Activity 8: Paper and pencils
Activity 9: Students' written work

The focus on language in literacy education still tends to concern verbal communication. What is neglected is a major way in which meaning is conveyed. In drama, we have the opportunity to draw our students' attention to what they are listening to with their eyes and seeing with their ears—that is, the dramatic *action*: the accumulation and movement of meanings; the action that lies *underneath* the words and the doing. Interpretation at this depth is a powerful exercising of communication skills; reading the body and writing with the body lead to an examination of human behavior in its broadest and richest sense (Miller and Saxton 2004b). When we fail to nurture these skills within the curriculum, we are negating a major means by which our students interpret the world in ways that are coherent for *them* (Gardner 1991). "Can we afford to lose," Neelands asks, "the ability to read and be sensitive to the signs that human beings offer each other?" (1993, 63).

Using children's picture books, we are "taking what we know in one communicative system and recasting it in terms of another system." In this way, "new signs and new forms of expression are created, and new knowledge generated." This is the "fundamental process of what it means to be literate" (Harste, Short, and Burke 1988, 353). As students work inside a story using what they know and who they are, their experiences can transform them into who they could be and what they could know. The levels on which signals are being sent and received are, in many ways, parallel to the ways in which the brain operates and develops: "We pull together fragments and find meaning by connecting many elements. And the force that sets the neurons firing and makes these connections possible is narrative" (Turner, cited in Fulford 1999, 83). Stimulated by a feeling engagement, entertained by curiosity, students find themselves practising their selves in new roles and in new lights in a *possible* world suggested by the story but owned and operated by them.

Being literate is to be able to participate in the multiliteracies of society (O'Mara 2003) as readers, observers, and communicators, processing and responding to meanings and practices that are personal, local, global and, often, all three at the same time. "Drama allows students to build a bridge between their own inner worlds and the external reality of other people, events, and ideas," writes John Hughes (1991, 37). In offering students opportunities to work with the multiple "languages" that effective literacies explore, we must not simply concentrate on what each language is, but on what they *do* and how they *shape* us and the world. Drama encourages this kind of self-literacy through its exercise of *all* the intelligences. Such literacy is, we suggest, crucial to the development of the whole person and, by extension, to the continued generation of healthy, literate, and democratic societies.

REFERENCES

Barone, Tom. 1990. "Using the Narrative Text as an Occasion for Conspiracy." In *Qualitative Inquiry in Education: The Continuing Debate*, edited by Eisner, E. and A. Peshkin, 305–326. New York: Teachers College Press.

Barron, Frank. 1988. "Putting Creativity to Work." In *The Nature of Creativity*, edited by R. Sternberg, 76–98. Cambridge: Cambridge University Press.

Benton, Michael. 1979. "Children's Responses to Stories." *Children's Literature in Education* 10 (2): 68–85.

Boal, Augusto. 1995. *The Rainbow of Desire*. Trans. by A. Jackson. London: Routledge.

Brook, Peter. 1987. The Shifting Point: Theatre, Film, Opera l946–l987. London: Harper & Rowe.

Brownlie, Faye, Susan Close, and Linda Wingren. 1988. *Reaching for Higher Thought*. Edmonton, AB: Arnold.

Bruner, Jerome. 1983. *Child's Talk: Learning to Use Language*. New York: WW Norton & Company.

Fulford, Robert. 1999. *The Triumph of Narrative: Storytelling in the Age of Mass Culture*. Toronto: Anansi.

Gardner, Howard. 1983. *Frames of Mind: The Theory of Multiple Intelligences*. New York: BasicBooks.

———. 1991. *The Unschooled Mind: How Children Think and How Schools Should Teach*. New York: BasicBooks.

Great Britain Central Advisory Council for Education (The Plowden Report). 1967. *Children and Their Primary Schools: A Report of the Central Advisory Council for Education (England)*. 2 vols. London: H.M. Stationery.

Hall, Nigel. 1998. "Real Literacy in a School Setting: Five-Year-Olds Take On the World." *The Reading Teacher* 52 (1): 8–17.

Harste, Jerome, Kathy Short, and Carolyn Burke. 1988. *Creating Classrooms for Authors*. Portsmouth, NH: Heinemann.

Hawkins, Margaret. 2004. "Researching English Language and Literacy Development in Schools." *Educational Researcher* 33 (3): 14–25.

Hughes, John. 1991. *Drama in Education: The State of the Art: An Australian Perspective*. Sydney, AU: New South Wales Educational Drama Association.

Manzo, A. V. 1969. "The ReQuest Procedure." *International Reading Association Journal of Reading* 13 (2): 126–132.

McEwan, Ian. 2001. "Comment: Special Report: Terrorism in the US." *The Guardian* (London), September 15.

Miller, Carole, and Juliana Saxton. 2004a. *Into the Story: Language in Action Through Drama*. Portsmouth, NH: Heinemann.

———. (2004b). Negotiating Meaning in the Living Classroom. Paper read at The International Consortium for Experiential Learning, September, Miami, Florida.

Morgan, Norah, and Juliana Saxton. 2000. 1998 Keynote Address: "Influences Around the 'Word.'" *Drama Matters: The Journal of the Ohio Drama Education Exchange* 4 (Summer): 7–20.

Neelands, Jonothan. 1993. "The Starry Messanger" (sic) (in which Galileo dismissed the myth that the moon was made of green cheese). In *Voices for Change*, edited by C. Lawrence, 52–64. Newcastle upon Tyne, UK: National Drama Publications.

O'Mara, JoAnne. 2003. "Repositioning Drama to Centre Stage: Drama, English, Text and Literacy." *NJ Drama Australia Journal* 27 (2): 17–27.

Preece, Alison. 2004. "Story Dramas as Scaffolds for Struggling Readers." *Disabled Readers Group Newsletter* 6 (2): 2–4.

Saul, John Ralston. 1995. *The Unconscious Civilization*. Concord, ON: Anansi.

Sawyer, R. Keith. 2004. "Creative Teaching: Collaborative Discussion as Disciplined Improvisation." *Educational Researcher* 33 (2): 12–20.

Schutz, Aaron. 2004. "Rethinking Domination and Resistance: Challenging Postmodernism." *Educational Researcher* 33 (1): 15–23.

Stewig, John. 1973, 1994. *Spontaneous Drama: A Language Art*. Columbus, OH: Charles E. Merrill Publishing Company.

Street, J. C., and Brian Street. 1991. "The Schooling of Literacy." In *Writing in the Community*, edited by D. Barton and R. Ivanic, 143–166. London: Sage.

Turner, Mark. 1996. *The Literary Mind: The Origins of Thought and Language*. Oxford: Oxford University Press.

3

The *Antigone* Project: Using Drama and Multiple Literacies to Support Print Literacy Among Youth

Kari-Lynn Winters, Theresa Rogers, and Andrew Schofield

Literacy and drama researcher David Booth (1994, 42) asks, "If narrative and drama give form to thought and feeling, can we make use of one to build the other? Can we use drama to clarify and strengthen the reading [and writing] of a story, and can we use the story to stimulate or enlighten the drama work?"

We sought to explore these questions with a group of students in an alternative Youth Literacy Project who actively participated in theatre games, improvisation, and role-playing and, later, created scenes from the play *Antigone* (originally written in 442 BC) (Sophocles 1949). Eventually they performed the various scenes; their processes and performances were captured on video. One student then produced a video "trailer" of an imagined upcoming film based on his interpretation of the play. These students were participating in an interdisciplinary unit that provided credits in English, communications, and film and TV—courses that count toward their secondary diplomas. They were also participating in a collaboratively designed arts and media-based Youth Literacy Project.

All of these students had fragile relationships with schooling: some had dropped out of traditional schools, some had been pushed out due to behavioral or other problems, and some had life circumstances that prevented them from continuing their education. Many of them also had low literacy skills as measured by standardized tests. The alternative Youth Literacy Project where this *Antigone* Project took place integrated the arts and media across subject areas, providing opportunities for students to re-engage in school in new ways. As Bruner (2002) argues, it is impossible to live outside of narratives that shape our consciousness and our identities. The *Antigone* Project created new narratives for the students to inhabit, if only temporarily. The drama approaches that were used supported creative thinking and a way for students to construct meaning and build connections with their worlds (Dyson 1997).

For several years, as researchers and teachers, we collaborated to develop a multiple literacies approach that would actively involve these reluctant youth, who struggle with print literacy and have been alienated from traditional schooling. We envisioned a place where students might engage in a range of print and nonprint or multimodal (Jewitt and Kress 2003) literacies, including visual arts, drama, theatre, photography, and video—a space where students could become codesigners of their own curricula. The students had opportunities to shape their representations of meaning from their life experiences and their interpretations of *Antigone*, and to construct knowledge and social skills they needed to participate in school and beyond. As Luke and Elkins (2002) argue, preparing today's culturally diverse youth for an increasingly complex information economy requires more than instruction in traditional print-based literacies. It includes the development of a range of multiple literacies and, we feel, opportunities to develop collaborative, imaginative, and critical literacy skills: the heart of the project.

In this chapter we illustrate how drawing on multiple literacies, particularly drama and other multimodal approaches, supports print-based literacies among adolescents, while providing spaces for them to express their narrative and critical understandings. Drama and other multimodal approaches are only rarely combined with or used to support print literacies in schools, yet they have rich potential to support youth who struggle to express or represent their ideas in print (Schofield and Rogers 2004). As multiple text forms, such as image, gesture, sound, and technology are infused into the curriculum, students have the potential to bridge their in- and out-of-school literacies (Goodman 2003; Jewitt and Kress 2003; Rogers and Schofield 2005). In this project, we foreground drama as a way to engage students, to link their drama processes to a range of multiple literacy practices, and to support their print literacy practices.

We begin by arguing that both print-based literacies and drama draw on imaginative, active, and social processes. We then present case studies of three adolescents who participated in the *Antigone* Project. We conclude that drama (and its extension into arts and video-making) and print literacy not only share similar learning dimensions, but also support each other, extending students' meaning-making within and beyond the curriculum.

DRAMA AND LITERACY AS IMAGINATIVE, ACTIVE, AND SOCIAL PROCESSES

Imaginative

Because drama works in the realm of the pretend, its very existence depends on imagination. O'Neill (1995) observes that "every work of art gives access to a self-contained imaginative universe, a dramatic 'elsewhere.'" Once actors and audiences are aware of the fictional world, they gain the capacity to explore a variety of new perspectives and construct new understandings of the drama's narrative and characters. For example, Rogers and O'Neill (1993) illustrate how drama in the literature classroom encourages students to draw on their own experiences and the literary text to create and enter new worlds, enabling them to question, challenge, and reflect on issues, dilemmas, and events suggested by the literary work. Students engaged in drama are simultaneously looking outward into the imaginary world and looking inward into the self.

Print literacy also involves imaginative dimensions. Bruner (1986) has argued that all narrative and interpretive knowing depends on the capacity to create and imagine a world. In ways similar to drama and other multiple literacy forms, reading is about crossing a gateway into the imagination. Indeed, Michael Benton (1979) characterizes the reader as a performer who builds a mental stage and fills it with people, scenes, and events that the text offers. When a student is engaged in reading, writing, viewing, or representing a text, he or she is at that moment a composer of ideas, a story-maker. It is this ability to enter into the story world and "transact" with it that draws on the imagination and strengthens a reader's (and, we would add, writer's) understanding of the text (Enciso 1992; Wilhelm 1997).

Active

Drama and literacy are also dynamic, active processes—not just physically, but also emotionally and cognitively. An actor acts on the world while actively participating in the imaginary narrative. A story develops, contexts change, and participants (actors and audience members) actively negotiate and compose meaning. This is why no two drama performances or "re-presentations" of meaning are the same, even when they are based on exactly the same printed text. As O'Neill (1995, 45) points out, drama requires "the participants to engage in active make-believe with regard to objects, actions and situations . . . [and] demand[s] a degree of interaction."

With each new performance, participants actively engage and reimagine the meaning of the drama in multimodal ways as the "bodies of the participants are stimulated as well as the minds" (Wagner 1998). To do this they draw on complex and alternating meaning-making modes, such as kinesthetic, aural, or visual modes of communication. These same meaning-making clues are often used in print literacy activities. For instance, young children often remember the alphabet through song; readers often stop to write their thoughts and hear and visualize storybook characters in their minds as they move through a story's setting. Some good readers and writers become so actively involved in the text that they are brought to tears, or laugh aloud, as they compose a tumultuous or delightful story. Reading and writing, like drama, have the potential to activate thinking in these dynamic, multimodal ways.

Social

Drama and literacy are both social processes, linking learning to participation in classroom communities. Participants of drama employ verbal and nonverbal communication systems, initiating and responding to meaningful ideas. Together, as students enter into their imagined contexts, they gain new insights while collectively negotiating meanings and investigating problems in spaces where my story is shaped by yours, and yours by mine. They leave the experience with new knowledge and the reminiscences of the powerful feelings they took from the drama and from their collectively negotiated narratives.

Individual readers and writers also bring to each text a social consciousness—a wealth of knowledge and experience of social situations, collaborative communication methods, and storytelling practices. We tell, remember, reconstruct, and apply stories from the places from which they come (Bruner 2002). The stories we've heard about ourselves in our early years and those we remember living through reappear in our own narratives, shaping our consciousness and our identity.

Because each of us has lived millions of stories (Leggo 2004), both our own and others', and because authors of narratives draw from this bank of stories when they construct anew, reading and writing becomes a social act. Bakhtin's (1981) work extends this perspective, arguing that all texts are dialogic, infused with a range of voices, perspectives, and points of view.

Participating in classroom literacy events is also a social process (Bloome 1986). We now understand that the array of literacy practices that take place in classrooms are wholly influenced by the institutional parameters of schooling and what it means "to do school" (Dyson 1984; Green, Kantor, and Rogers 1990). Current views of literacy situate print literacy practices within the social structures in which they are embedded and which they help to shape (Barton and Hamilton 2000). In this way, literacy practices connect people to one another, straddling individual and social worlds.

The challenge for us in the *Antigone* Project was to capture the ways in which the students drew on the imaginative, active, and social processes of drama, together with other multimodal approaches, to support their print literacy practices and abilities, to negotiate with us and with each other in social contexts, and to critically reflect on the stories they were telling and the skills they were bringing to the Project.

THE *ANTIGONE* PROJECT

The Youth Literacy Project (YLP), situated in an alternative school in Surrey, British Columbia, offers an individualized program that supports the curriculum through adaptive instruction, teacher or peer tutoring, and multiple literacies. Approximately thirty-two students, ranging in age from fifteen to nineteen years, attend the YLP. Although many of these youth read and write below grade level and/or face additional challenges—such as alienation from schooling, drug abuse, violence, hunger, and homelessness—the multidisciplinary approach of this program helps to motivate the students and keep them in school. This approach has been developed during a three-year collaborative project between the school and the University of British Columbia. The goal of the project was to include arts, media, and multidisciplinary practices to connect literacy to the lives of youth and to support their in- and out-of-school literacy development (Schofield and Rogers 2004).

During the second year, we collaborated on the *Antigone* Project, including the implementation of a series of theatre and drama techniques and activities, some of which were designed to address Provincially prescribed learning outcomes and some that were co-constructed by the teacher-researchers. In total, seventeen students participated in the *Antigone* Project. Students engaged in theatre games (October to November), improvisation (November), role dramas (December), script or scene building (December–January), playmaking or theatre rehearsals (February to March), and storyboarding and filmmaking (October through March). These activities are defined and further explained below:

- *Theatre Games.* We began the *Antigone* Project with a number of theatre games recommended in the Provincial curriculum guidelines. According to Spolin (1963, 382), a theatre game is defined as an accepted group activity that is limited by rules and group agreement, parallels the theatre experience, and includes the fun, spontaneity, and joy that accompanies games. These cooperative games were more than just warm-ups. Consistent class attendance demonstrated how these games encouraged participant motivation. In addition, the theatre games seemed to help students develop performance skills (e.g., reacting without hesitation; incorporating movement with vocalization; developing an awareness of inner emotions), while providing opportunities where the students could respond to one another. Some examples of theatre games that were played included "Yes, let's," "What are you doing?" and "Pass the imagined prop."
- *Improvisation.* From the theatre games we moved into improvisation, performing spontaneous and scriptless scenes that were created entirely by the group of performing actors. Unlike theatre games, our improvised scenes included an audience (teachers and other students who were not participating in that particular scene). Improvisation provided more opportunities for team and performance skill-building. In addition, it gave students a chance to begin storytelling and building imagined contexts. Following the project, one student said this about the improvisation: "I'm not that good at writing. But with acting, just like with pictures, I could write a story, and the others could understand it better too." Some of the improvisation titles included "Bus stop," "Elevator," and "Party quirks."
- *Role Dramas.* Following the improvisation, we introduced the play *Antigone* and developed role dramas: the students co-constructed the story, actively identifying with imagined roles in the drama to explore and reflect on the play's issues, events, and relationships (O'Neill and Lambert 1991). The focus of our role-plays was to explore issues of betrayal, social status, and suicide in *Antigone*, transposing these into our modern-day

society and drawing on the students' lived experiences. By highlighting the intersections of their own worlds and the world of the story, students appeared better able to engage with and comprehend the play itself (Booth 1994). One student said, "Like Malcolm X, they [the performers] made it [*Antigone*] more modern, then it was more interesting."
- *Script or Scene Building.* Using the content we had gained from the role dramas, we revised and rewrote the script of *Antigone*, cutting scenes, adding story details and scenes, and working through difficult portions of the play. This creative writing process, facilitated through the role drama exercises, was based on the play itself and also upon the students' lives and imaginations. For example, one student thought that the play needed a modern-day narrator to give details about the original story and to clarify some of the contemporary connections he had discovered by working through the play: "It needed some explanation, so I decided there needed to be a narrator."
- *Playmaking or Theatre Rehearsal.* This was the process of rehearsing and presenting scenes from the play. Its focus was on bringing the story off the page, developing characters, and creating story events through blocking and dialogue. One student in particular really benefited from this phase, saying "It makes more sense [to act it out], rather than just reading the play." At this point, with many curricular goals met, the playmaking component of the course concluded and we shifted focus to storyboarding and filmmaking.
- *Storyboarding and Filmmaking.* Throughout this whole school year, for their film and television credit, students were also simultaneously creating storyboards, music videos, and short films. These storyboards and films provided other media through which they could visually represent stories. One student, Jason (discussed later in the case studies), while performing the play, couldn't stop thinking like a film director. "I just had this idea. Then the play just got cancelled. I had to take over. I looked at [the process] from a film director's point of view." As a way to get closure on the project (it was his final year in the school) and to "put [his] vision into it," he created a storyboard and then a film trailer for his imagined upcoming film.

During these various stages and drama activities, each of the students who participated in the project wove together multiple literacies—including drama and print literacies—in unique ways. We focus on three students, highlighting their negotiations of meaning, how they drew upon the imaginative, active, and social dimensions of the project, and what they gained from this multiple literacy approach.

Engaging in Multiple Forms of Meaning-Making: Sam, Joey, and Jason

In order to take a closer look at the multiple literacy practices of the students in the project, we observed them and kept field notes and journals, videotaped their drama work, and looked at various documents, such as reading evaluations and writing products. We then selected three students, each with a very different literacy profile, and traced each one's participation in the project.

Sam As an already prolific poet, Sam related well to his peers and to his contemporary youth culture. He enjoyed being with his friends or writing raw, unedited poetry. Some of his pieces had been submitted for publication, but most sat dormant on the scraps of paper on which he wrote. When his teachers suggested that he revisit his poetry or publish it, he was resistant. Revising on paper, he admitted, "is boring" because "it takes less of an artistic feel" and because "you do it by yourself." Needless to say, many of his thought-provoking poems remained unrevised and unpublished.

Sam came to the *Antigone* Project interested and ready to work; he had taken drama classes at his previous secondary school. He believed that drama would be fun, but also something that he could do easily to earn credits in communication, English, and film and TV courses. During the theatre games and improvisation sections of the project, Sam participated eagerly, adding excitement and humor to many of the scenes. During one improvisation Sam had the whole audience laughing. What stands out about that particular scene was that Sam only spoke one word over and over again. By using movement and the word "ding," he and another actor created a narrative about two very different people stuck in an elevator. Sam's character was impatient and rather annoying, while the other student's character was calm and tolerant. Throughout the improvised scene, Sam's character rubbed off on the other student's character, moving him from calm to more irritable. Scenes like these and others demonstrated how Sam seemed to love the spotlight and also how much he liked working collaboratively with a partner or group.

Then came the role drama. By December, students were asked to think about the story of *Antigone* and to transfer some of the story events to a modern-day context. Sam remained actively engaged in this process. He offered input about creating a community of drug dealers. Sam drew a connection between *Antigone* and a modern-day context, noting that in both there was a social chain of command. In other words, King Creon was similar to a leader of a drug cartel, for both have power and people working for them. In this way, Creon's sentries and messengers were similar to street dealers in that they are also told what to do.

Two changes occurred during the scene-building sessions. First, as in his poetry, Sam began to think metaphorically about *Antigone*'s themes (e.g., suicide, betrayal, and social power), and easily transferred them to a modern context. His thinking about these scenes in this comparative way allowed him to better understand the script, for he was bringing his own experience and knowledge to the text. Second, he used the negotiations of meaning that he constructed around *Antigone* and applied them back to his life and to his poetry. Traces of the content or conflict of these scenes were being transferred to the snippets of paper he scrawled his poetry on and left about the room:

> *I will not tiptoe through life to arrive safely at death.*
> *Life lives in your blood, not your bullet.*
> *Love lives in your heart, not in your battle.*
> *Through my heart I feel and cry.*
> *Through your smile I learn to fly.*

Yet these poetic insights were still not being revisited; instead, they were left on the table or floor and rarely given another thought. A chain of events during the playmaking section of the project is what changed this. It was during this part of the project that Sam began to extend his revising skills.

First, Sam was not chosen to play Haemon or Creon, yet he wanted a spotlight role. He made it clear, by being resistant and talking openly to his peers, that he "wasn't pleased" that "the good parts had been taken." In addition, he felt that the story was not clear enough for a modern audience; "it needed some explanation." For these reasons, Sam approached Andrew, asking if he could create his own narrator role. Andrew not only agreed; he worked closely with Sam, helping him to write the part. They worked scene by scene, inserting the modern-day narrator's role into the script. These inserts, much like Sam's writing, were also raw and poetic:

> *Two dead soldiers, one filled grave.*
> *Antigone's blood bleeds in hate and smashes with rage.*
> *But her heart keeps beating. Our feelings meet with her pain.*

> *To her life, she kisses her soul to rest.*
> *Because life is not what you make it.*
> *It is what you leave it to be.*

Although these additional inserts looked good to Sam on paper, it wasn't until they were performed in the group space that Sam realized they didn't seem to fit well with the traditional script. "They were too poetic," said Sam, "and they took away from the overall mood and atmosphere of the play." Hence, Sam consciously began to remake his revisions and additions so that they would better correspond with this dramatic genre.

He decided to change the tone of the piece. Instead of being only the poet, Sam also became the informant, the storyteller. His lines began to fill in the story, describing the setting, giving his impressions of the characters, providing information about previous events, and explaining the meaning he constructed about each scene. He chose to form this role using modern language so that the audience could easily relate to the story. By watching and taking suggestions from the actors, and by filling in significant historical and narrative facts, he began to rewrite his role. Throughout the rehearsals he reshaped and edited his writing again and again until it suited the play and the moment, as the following excerpt exemplifies:

"Welcome. I am about to show you a story that takes place in ancient Greece, yet reflects the present. It presents the problems, the successes of our day. The play begins in the time of Creon, with two sisters in the morning fog. One sister believes that a woman has the right to go against the king. But the other sister has a difference of opinion when the king buries one of her brothers yet lays a law to leave the other brother to the animals. Two dead soldiers, one filled grave. And now, our feature presentation."

As we argued earlier, drama, like writing, is a social process; good actors and good writers consider their audience. Writers compose material that can be constructed by a reader. For Sam, it was this awareness of the audience that made him realize how important editing is. "I was constantly researching," he said later, "taking in the atmosphere, and looking at the reactions of the actors. I listened to what the directors [Andrew, Kari, Ginger (another teacher) and Theresa] were saying. That really helped me to remake the script."

In the end, the narrator role that he composed not only gave Sam opportunities to write in a different genre than he was used to; it gave him structure within a collaborative setting, and it encouraged him to reflect on his writing. When we called attention to his script revisions and compared it to a piece of his unedited poetry, he seemed surprised. "Oh yeah," he said, "this [drama] piece is more polished." When asked why he was able to edit during the drama but not with his poetry, he responded: "There was more action. It's easier. You can imagine the vibe better. There's also a whole group with you. It's just easier; you didn't have to twist my arm." Here, drama, which added a social dimension to Sam's writing, supported his composition and revision processes. The drama enabled him to authentically call upon his editorial skills while strengthening his writing.

Joey Joey came to the project with different strengths and weaknesses. Unlike Sam, Joey was a reluctant writer and struggled to comprehend beyond a literal level when reading. Although he liked to read skateboarding magazines, any other reading or writing task was considered a chore. When Kari evaluated his literacy skills, he struggled to decode and comprehend text at the secondary levels. His writing was filled with simple sentences and invented spelling. Sometimes the grammar was incoherent. Joey instinctively knew this. "I am not a good reader or writer," he admitted repeatedly.

However, Joey had good instincts for performing, and this became clear immediately. He excelled during the theatre games and improvisation sessions. He clearly portrayed his characters through both movement and voice. Although he was content to share the spotlight, his quiet presence often became the focus of each improvisation he participated in. In one scene he played a smiley, confused man waiting for the bus; he made occasional comments about how cool everyone was and how nice their names sounded. His character, although subtle, added humor and a story line to the scene. His peers recognized his skill and often asked him to join their groups. And during the auditions, he landed one of the lead roles—King Creon.

Joey continued to actively participate in discussions during the role drama and scene-building sessions, but never volunteered to write anything down. In fact, when it came to reading and writing, Joey disengaged. As we moved into playmaking sessions, which required the students to work from a script, we noticed that Joey was falling further behind. Not only was he reluctant to read aloud, stammering and struggling to pronounce the words, he was also grappling to understand what was happening onstage. He admitted that he was "lost," and could not describe what was happening in the play. Although his peers were patient and understanding, he felt embarrassed reading in front of them. Here is a transcript (February) of an unrehearsed scene:

"Laws were made. You broke them (*pause*). You, but then (*pause*) you'll do it and again (*pause*). You (*stammered*) brag about it then (*stammered*) you laugh (*shakes head, pauses*). Yes, the other girl (*pause*) I (*stammered*) I, oh (*looks closely at paper*) I held (*pause*) equally responsible (*squints*). I held her equally responsible for plotting the burial (pause). Summon her here immediately (*pause*) . . ."

We began to tutor him more extensively, focusing mostly on the plot and on his character's story. We also helped him with word analysis skills, and with the script vocabulary. We worked with him individually and within the group setting.

Even though it was difficult for Joey, he persisted, participating in the drama and wanting to be the best King Creon he could be. He practiced his scenes and worked on his lines constantly. The drama context allowed him to reread a piece of text and to physically negotiate his understanding of the script. By March, after working through the first half of the play, he had improved his fluency and his comprehension of the play. Here he is reading the same passage later:

"Laws were made. You broke them. Then to do it again and again (*pause*) bragging about it and laughing (*pause*). Yes, the other girl (*pause*) I held her equally responsible for plotting the burial (*pause*). Summon her here immediately (*pause*)."

Joey could now summarize the play. He talked about the two sisters, about the death of Antigone's brother and about how she wanted to bury him. He told us that Antigone had gone against Creon's orders and that was why she had been sentenced to death. Yet, he still struggled to make sense of what happened at the end of the play—especially with the scenes he had not yet rehearsed. By actively embodying his character's story—living inside his character's community and "being the book" (Wilhelm 1997)—he was more able to make connections with the play. He could participate in the classroom in ways that he couldn't have without the drama.

The active nature of this drama project, and the additional support provided by his teachers, his peers, and the researchers, allowed Joey to actively imagine and embody the words of the script. Much like a sculptor, he could now understand his materials (the words) and could shape them into meaningful forms. Because he had physically worked with these words, actively constructing and negotiating their meaning, Joey strengthened his fluency and comprehension and could participate more fully in the life of the classroom. When we asked how drama supported his print literacy skills, he said, "A picture tells a thousand words. I kind of have bad reading and writing, but I can show a picture, or act, and the person I show [it to] understands it. And then I understand it better too."

Jason Jason would be considered a conscientious student. Although his grades were average, he gave his projects (both in and out of school) considerable thought and attention. This became evident in his interviews as he reflected upon his process. "I knew I had the [acting] skills, but I needed to work on showing emotions. I thought about it a lot. I just slept on the play."

Jason mentioned that he came to this project with shyness and hesitation. Nevertheless, he jumped right in, participating wholeheartedly in the project. "I had to overcome [my shyness]," he said, "be open, be comfortable with an audience. The more characters [you portray] the better it is."

During each session, Jason was engaged. He became a composer of ideas, a story-maker who moved through the drama activities, demonstrating success in all of its forms. He took in each piece of the project, building on the knowledge he established for each text form and then transferring it to his next literacy event. "I want to put it all together," he said later. "I struggle to read and write sometimes, but with movies, then I totally understand. Music too. Themes can be known through the beats, the words. I want to put it all together—my life experiences."

Jason relied on his visual and spatial imagination, envisioning how a scene could look even before it was created: "Even though it was written, I have to visualize it." This was especially true during the role drama and scene-building sessions. Jason had a vision of how the play could be performed, and how it could be contextualized for the present day. During the role-play sessions, he offered suggestions about the themes of the play: "Oh, I know. Gangs, encounters, then someone dies." He went on to discuss the funeral and the friendships that could develop between the gangs.

As he shared these ideas with his peers, he spoke as though he were the director. Later he mentioned that by taking the director's point of view, the drama became more meaningful to him. "I had to be the boss" he said. "I had to put my vision into it."

Jason's ability to visualize transferred to his print literacy process as well. When asked how drama and multiple forms of literacy helped him both in and out of school, he stated that he became better at understanding scripts and at writing. "Reading is boring. But if it is acted out, you're like, Wow! It's different! Regular classrooms should think about bringing it off the page—to show it, to use it!"

Beyond the *Antigone* Project, Jason decided to storyboard and create a film trailer on his own time. "I thought making a movie would be great 'cause these guys are shy too. Just acting it out in front of me—it really helped Joey to say his lines like he meant them." Jason used his spatial imagination when retelling the story, setting up complicated film shots to demonstrate his vision. In his words, he put his own "vision" into it. When asked about how he imagined this movie trailer, he replied, "I didn't want any plain front-view shots. I wanted to make the camera angles interesting. I cut scenes. I did face shots, then larger shots, over-the-shoulder shots, underneath shots. One shot is boring. I just want to make stories about people—real people." Here Jason is demonstrating his understanding of filmic space. In order to suggest "real people" in real space within the two-dimensional space of the screen, he understood that he needed to provide a range of shots from various angles.

During this project, Jason drew upon the imaginative dimensions of storytelling (through print, drama, and film), helping us to understand how multiple literacies support print literacy. Jason was a story-maker, who, when given multimedia tools (drama, film) strengthened and displayed his narrative vision. Later, Jason extended his comprehension of the script by creating a striking trailer for the upcoming film of *Antigone* based on scenes performed by his peers and filmed under his direction.

Unfortunately, a planned public performance of the reworked play was cancelled because Andrew felt that several of the students were not making the necessary commitment to the project to make it work. As we mentioned earlier, being in school and working collaboratively is a struggle for students who have not been successful in such settings. Encouraging collaboration is an ongoing mission of the program.

CONCLUSION

We have emphasized that drama and literacy are similar meaning-making and complementary processes that are imaginative, active, and social. Together they can serve to support and reinforce meaning-making in multiple ways for learners. When given a chance to express themselves in multimodal ways and to transform ideas into an art form—not reducible to words, but one that can be read by others—students gain motivation for learning and improved collaborative meaning-making skills (Gallas 1994; Jewitt and Kress 2003; Wilhelm 1997).

In this project, we saw how students were drawing on their background knowledge and experiences and were composing, decoding, visualizing, revising, and negotiating social relationships in the interfaces of drama, literacy, and multimedia. We found that for these students in the Youth Literacy Project, drama and literacy did indeed become mutual partners in extending the students' learning and offered opportunities for them ". . . to imagine possibilities that are not now, but which might become" (Eisner 1998, 99).

At the intersection of these meaning-making approaches, the students were able to bring their cultural experiences to comment upon and critique the stories being told. For Sam, *Antigone* came alive in the metaphoric spaces between contemporary street life and the power structures of Thebes. For Joey, performance allowed him to enter into the story world enough to imagine Antigone's powerlessness at the hands of Joey's own character. Jason's director's understanding of story allowed him to imagine a present-day context in which a funeral might reconcile previous enemies. Regardless of their skill level, these students were able to appropriate texts and media for their own ends, engage in multiple literacies as critical social practices (Street 1995), and imagine new possibilities for themselves.

REFERENCES

Bakhtin, Mikhail. 1981. *The Dialogic Imagination*. Austin, TX: University of Austin Press.

Barton, David, and Mary Hamilton. 2000. "Literacy Practices." In *Situated Literacies: Reading and Writing in Context*, edited by D. Barton, M. Hamilton, and R. Ivanic. 7–15. London: Routledge.

Benton, Michael. 1979. "Children's Responses to Stories." *Children's Literature in Education* 10(2): 68–86.

Bloome, David. 1986. "Reading as a Social Process." *Language Arts* 62(2): 134–142.

Booth, David. 1994. *Story Drama: Reading, Writing and Roleplaying Across the Curriculum*. Markham, ON: Pembroke Publishers.

Bruner, Jerome. 1986. *Actual Minds, Possible Worlds*. Cambridge, MA: Harvard University Press.

———. 2002. *Making Stories: Law, Literature, Life*. Cambridge, MA: Harvard University Press.

Dyson, Anne Haas. 1984. "Learning to Write/Learning to Do School." *Research in the Teaching of English* 18(3): 233–264.

_____. 1997. *Writing Superheroes: Contemporary Childhood, Popular Culture, and Classroom Literacy*. New York: Teachers College Press.

Eisner, Elliot. 1998. *The Kinds of Schools We Need: Personal Essays*. Portsmouth, NH: Heinemann.

Enciso, Patricia. 1992. "Creating the Story World: A Case Study of a Young Reader's Engagement Strategies and Stances." In *Reader Stance and Literary Understanding: Exploring the Theories, Research and Practice*, edited by J. Many and C. Cox, 75–102. Norwood, NJ: Ablex Publishing Corporation.

Gallas, Karen. 1994. *The Languages of Learning: How Children Talk, Write, Dance, Draw, and Sing Their Understanding of the World*. New York: Teachers College Press.

Green, Judith, Rebecca Kantor, and Theresa Rogers. 1990. "Exploring the Complexity of Language and Learning." In *Educational Values and Cognitive Instructional Implications for Reform*, edited by L. Idol and B. Jones, 333–364. Mahwah, NJ: Erlbaum Associates.

Goodman, Steven. 2003. *Teaching Youth Media: A Critical Guide to Literacy, Video Production, and Social Change*. New York: Teachers College Press.

Jewitt, Carey, and Gunther Kress, eds. 2003. *Multimodal Literacy*. Vol. 4. New York: Peter Lang.

Leggo, Carl. 2004. "Tangled Lines: On Autobiography and Poetic Knowing." In *Provoked by Art: Theorizing Arts-informed Research*. Edited by A. Cole, L. Neilsen, J. G. Knowles, and T. Luciana, 18–35. Halifax, Nova Scotia: Backalong Books.

Luke, Allan, and John Elkins. 2002. "Towards a Critical, Worldly Literacy." *Journal of Adolescent and Adult Literature* 45(8): 668–673.

O'Neill, Cecily. 1995. *Drama worlds: A framework for process drama*. Portsmouth, NH: Heinemann.

O'Neill, Cecily, and Allan Lambert. 1991. *Drama Structures*. Portsmouth, NH: Heinemann.

Rogers, Theresa, and Cecily O'Neill. 1993. "Creating Multiple Worlds: Drama, Language, and Literary Response." In *Exploring Texts*, edited by G. Newell and R. Durst, 69–89. Norwood, MA: Christopher-Gordon.

Rogers, Theresa, and Andrew Schofield. 2005. "Things Thicker than Words: Portraits of Youth Multiple Literacies in an Alternative Secondary Program." In *Portraits of Literacy Across Families, Schools and Communities*, edited by J. Anderson, M. Kendrick, T. Rogers, and S. Smythe, 205–220. Mahwah, NJ: Erlbaum Associates.

Rosenblatt, Louise. 1978. *The Reader, the Text, the Poem: The Transactional Theory of the Literary Work*. Carbondale, IL: Southern Illinois University Press.

Schofield, Andrew, and Theresa Rogers. 2004. "At Play in Fields of Ideas: Teaching, Curriculum, and the Lives and Multiple Literacies of Youth. *Journal of Adolescent and Adult Literacy* 48: 238–248.

Sophocles. 1949. *The Oedipus Cycle*. San Diego: Harcourt Brace and Company.

Spolin, Viola. 1963. *Improvisation for the Theater*. Evanston, IL: Northwestern University Press.

Street, Brian. 1995. *Social Literacies: Critical Approaches to Literacy in Development, Ethnography and Education*. New York: Longman.

Wagner, Betty Jane. 1998. *Educational Drama and Language Arts: What Research Shows*. Portsmouth, NH: Heinemann.

Wilhelm, Jeffrey. 1997. *"You Gotta Be the Book": Teaching Engaged and Reflective Reading with Adolescents*. New York: Teachers College Press.

4

Identity and Imagination of Immigrant Children: Creating Common Place Locations in Literary Interpretation

Carmen L. Medina

In this chapter I present my work with a group of recently immigrated fifth-grade students. We explored Latina/o children's literature through multiple sign systems such as drama, talk, and visual sketches. I used Sumara's notions of "common place location" in literary interpretation as a framework to interpret how, as the children shifted from one sign system to the other, they interpreted text and identity, creating rich and complex personal, imaginative, and cultural responses. The combination of sign systems and literary and identity explorations in the students' responses provided a location where multiple literacies were mediated to enact multiple forms of knowledge.

CREATING COMMON PLACE LOCATIONS IN LITERARY ENGAGEMENT

The recent work of Sumara (1996, 2001, 2002) in literary interpretation provides a productive framework from which to understand the ways that experience, identity, and literary response connect. According to Sumara, by employing particular interpretative practices in our relationships with literary texts, a space is created that "can become a productive site for the continued interpretation of culture and the way culture is historically influenced" (2002, 29). This notion of how history and culture influences our interpretation of texts provides a rich lens to look at the relationship between texts and readers in complex ways. In what he calls a "common place location," a space is created between reader and text for ongoing literary interpretation that allows readers to self-identify with characters and plot rather than locating interpretative truths within the text. Similar to forms of reader response theory (Rosenblatt 1978), Sumara argues that the meaning readers construct is not located in the text but instead in the relationship between reader and text: "The place of mediation is not in the text but rather in the relationship that is formed between the reader and the text—in the interstices" (2002, 48–49). Furthermore, he challenges us to think that each space or location created between reader and texts is always different and never looks the same as we read and reread, interpret and reinterpret literary works and our life experiences within those moments. These dynamic and constantly changing relationships do not only have an impact on the ways we read and interpret texts but also in the construction of the readers' self-identities: "These activities illuminate the processes by which human beings experience a sense of personal identity and, importantly, how these experiences are necessarily organized by remembered, currently lived, and imagined identifications and relationships" (2001, 168).

Sumara invites literature practitioners to explore forms of literary response that create interpretative sites "where readers have an opportunity to create an intertext that collects traces of various representations of their in- and out-of-text experiences" (2001, 173). In this chapter I use Sumara's notions to argue how, through readers' engagement in multimodal interpretations of texts, such as talk, visual representations and drama, they create a common place location to explore a sense of history, self, and imagination. The students, through these literary engagements, bring their linguistic, cultural, and personal resources to make sense of particular literary experiences in the classroom.

MULTIPLE SIGN SYSTEMS AS COMMON PLACE LOCATIONS

The use of multiple sign systems (e.g., visual communication, drama communication, and oral communication) as literary response have been one area of interest among literacy practitioners (Short, Harste, and Burke 1996; Berghoff et al. 2000; Siegel 1995; Rogers and O'Neill 1993; Medina 2004; Enciso and Edmiston 1997). As theories of multiple literacies (The New London Group 2000) become increasingly popular, literacy educators are becoming even more aware and interested in the ways to design and redesign different types of "texts" across sign systems in different cultural contexts. In literary response, through multiple sign systems, spaces are created in classrooms to provide opportunities to respond to texts in ways that represent "a full repertoire of meaning making resources" (Jewitt et al. 2001, 5). By exploring a repertoire of ways to make meaning, children's relationships with texts will not be limited to reading and writing; the children also are encouraged to engage in other forms of communicating ideas.

Providing curricular engagements using multiple sign systems such as drama, movement, visual arts, and others becomes a productive site to represent knowledge in a variety of forms. As children are invited to respond to texts through diverse signs, they begin to articulate multiple ways in which they perceive texts and self. Through talk, visual arts, and drama, among others, readers interpret texts in ways that become complex common place locations for literary interpretation. Furthermore, as readers shift from one sign system to another, they design forms of interpretation that represent diverse aspects and moments of self, identity, and culture.

In making the connections between common place locations and multiple sign systems, I share how I used different sign systems as curricular engagements to explore the picture book *My Diary from Here to There/My Diario de Aquí Hasta Allá* by Latina writer Amada Pérez (2002). As children shifted from literature discussion to drama to visual representations, they interpreted texts and self, creating a common place location where they explored the complex relationship between the issues in the text and the histories and present circumstances of their own lives and those of others.

A VIEW FROM A CLASSROOM

The repertoire of engagements I present here were part of a larger ethnographic study that examined children's responses to literature written by Latina/o writers. In this chapter, I share my work with a small group of five students in a fifth-grade English as a Second Language (ESL) classroom. The students had moved within approximately a year or two from Mexico (four students) and El Salvador (one student) to the midwestern United States. Spanish was the dominant language for all the students in the small group, but their schooling experiences were largely dominated by English—a tension that was constantly present and revealed at different moments throughout our experience together.

In collaboration with the classroom teacher, I developed a set of curricular engagements to explore *My Diary from Here to There/Mi Diario de Aquí Hasta Allá*. In this bilingual picture book the main character, Amanda, tells about her experience of leaving her house in Mexico and moving to Los Angeles, California. Amanda shares her journal "from here to there" throughout the journey. She narrates her siblings' reactions to the moment when her parents informed the children they were leaving Mexico. After packing, the journey began by going to Mexicali, a town close to the border. The father first crossed the border to find a job as a migrant farmworker and worked to get green cards for the family. Back in Mexicali the family stayed at a cousin's home and anxiously awaited letters and news from the father. Once the father obtained green cards, the children and mother crossed the border and their lives began in Los Angeles. The story ends with Amanda writing her first diary entry in Los Angeles.

The story, situated in a border literature/*literatura fronteriza* narrative tradition (Calderón and Saldívar 1991), in many ways resembled the students' experiences of border crossing. Therefore the book worked as a powerful text for the students to bring past and present histories to their literary interpretations. In the next sections I describe the ways each sign system created a location for literary and self-interpretation similar to those described by Sumara. The first common place location I share is an example of "talk" in a literature discussion; the second example is visual "sketches" based on the students' interpretations of the story; and the third is a drama structure that explored the characters' experiences after they arrived in Los Angeles. For each common place location described I share an example of the students' work.

Common Place Location #1: Exploring Texts and Identity Through Talk

Our reading of *My Diary From Here to There/Mi Diario de Aquí Hasta Allá* was framed as a literature discussion. In order to facilitate the discussion we read parts of the book aloud each day. We wrote down questions and ideas that came to our minds throughout the reading. Those questions, connections, and ideas became the springboard to our discussions. The students brought multiple personal experiences, particularly related to notions of border crossing, to the table. In the following example we read the beginning of the book, in which the parents tell Amanda and her brothers that they are leaving Mexico to live in Los

A VIEW FROM A CLASSROOM   57

Angeles. After reading this section Francisco (all names are pseudonyms) initiates the conversation by sharing a personal thought.

[I read the part when the parents tell the children they are leaving.] (In this small group discussion the students and I spoke Spanish and my translations are in italics.)

FRANCISCO: (En voz muy baja.) Cuando yo vine [para los Estados Unidos] me puse a llorar.
(In a very low voice.) When I came [to the United States] I began to cry.
CARMEN: ¿Como?
What?
IVONNE: Que cuando vino se puso a llorar.
That when he came he began crying.
FRANCISCO: No (sonríe)
No (smiles)
YOLANDA: A veces si da tristeza.
Sometimes it does make you sad.
DIEGO: A veces.
Sometimes.
JUAN: Pero a veces no. A veces te da rabia.
But sometimes it doesn't. Sometimes it makes you angry.
YOLANDA: Cuando veníamos para acá yo no quería venir.
When we came here I didn't want to come.
IVONNE: Yo tenia miedo por lo que pasaba en la tele.
I was scared because of what happened on the TV.
CARMEN: ¿Que pasaba en la tele?
What happened on the TV?
IVONNE: Que cuando pasaran, tenían que correr y todo eso pero no fue así.
That when they passed [the border], they had to run and all of that. But it wasn't like that.
FRANCISCO: Yo corrí.
I ran.
JUAN: Yo me vine en avión y cuando vienes en avión, se mueve el avión y te da dolor de cabeza. Después te ponen la comida pero la tienes que apretar un poco para que cuando vaya el avión pa' arriba no se te caiga tu comida. Y el jugo sabía hasta un poco amargo y le dije que me hiciera un café.
I came by airplane and when you come by airplane, the airplane moves and you get a headache. Then they give you the food but you

have to hold it a little bit tight so it won't fall when the plane is going up. And the juice tasted sour and I told them to make me a coffee.
YOLANDA: Yo cuando vine de México vine en avión y como es en Veracruz se veían todas las montañas.
When I came from México, I came by airplane and because it was on Veracruz you could see all the mountains.
IVONNE: Yo no. Yo pase por el carro por la línea.
I didn't. I passed on the car through the border.
[Everybody talks at the same time]
JUAN: (A Yolanda) ¿Verdad que se veía el mundo? En Veracruz se veía bien bonito porque . . . ¿Como se llama? Como un pedazo de Veracruz queda un poco a fuera del agua y cuando fuimos para arriba, se veían las montañas, se veían las nubes, se veía un poco verde y el agua.
(Addressing Yolanda) Isn't it true that you could see the world? In Veracruz you could see it very pretty because . . . how do you say it? Like a piece of Veracruz is a little bit outside of the water and when we went up, you could see the mountains, you could see the clouds, you could see a little green and the water.
(My Diary: Discussion: 1-20-04)

In this particular literature discussion, the children shared a diverse set of experiences of border crossing. Their explorations in many ways resembled those represented in Latina writer Anzaldúa's (1987) theoretical explorations of border crossing. According to Anzaldúa, "the border" is not just a geographical space but also a physical, emotional, and social space. The children in their discussion talked about all of these aspects—geographical, physical, emotional, and social—as they related past and present experiences amongst themselves. Francisco began this conversation by stating, a little embarrassed, that he cried. His comment was supported by Yolanda's, as well as Diego's, reaffirmation that crossing the border and coming to a new place is sometimes sad. Juan added a new perspective and brought his feelings of occasional anger in coming to a new place. Their descriptions showed the emotional load carried by immigrant children in the process of coming to a new country. A common place location was created to interpret the characters' and the students' emotional past and present histories with border crossing. Furthermore, this common place location worked to explore the multiple social dynamics embedded in border crossing— particularly how the students established differences in the ways they came to the United States. This aspect of the dialogue created a social and geographical location where there was a clear difference between those students who entered the United States by plane and with some form of residency documentation and those who crossed the border hiding from immigration authorities. This dichotomy was recurrent in their discussions. While Yolanda and Juan concentrated on describing the geography of Veracruz and the airplane trip, Juan, Francisco, and Ivonne talked about hiding and the fear. And in Ivonne's case, she made a connection to how her fear of border crossing was shaped by television media.

Common Place Location #2: Exploring text Through Visual Sketches

The second curricular engagement we used to explore this text was "sketch to stretch" (Short, Harste, and Burke 1996). Using paper cuts as the medium, each student created a representation of the story and wrote a description of what the sketch meant. In the following excerpt, Diego wrote about his sketch:

> Mi arte me recuerda cuando yo cruce la frontera. Mi arte significa cuando Amanda cruzo la frontera.
>
> *My art reminds me when I crossed the border. My art means when Amanda crossed the border.*

Diego was a student from El Salvador who, at the time of the study, had recently crossed the USA/Mexico border. His experiences crossing the border were at the center of the literature discussion but also in his engagement in developing his sketch. An analysis of his paper-cuts sketch suggested how he created a common place location to analyze the text and his experiences, as well as the present classroom context as a community of people who brought diverse experiences crossing borders. Very similar to the illustrations on the cover of the book *My Diary from Here to There/Mi Diario de Aquí Hasta Allá*, Diego represented the house in Mexico with a car on the road leaving to cross the border. He added labels to his sketch naming important elements in crossing the border. These elements included the United States, the border, a car, people, and water, making reference to the Rio Grande between Mexico and the United States. Diego also brought an interesting connection between the text, his present experiences, and the rest of the class when he labeled what seemed to be "the border" on the water with the names of the different countries where those in the classroom

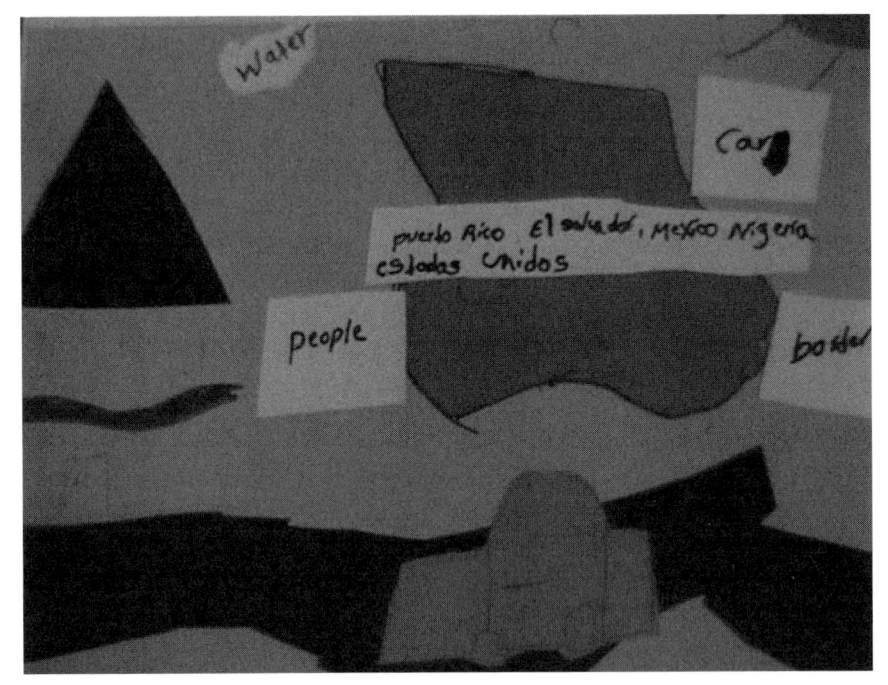

60 IDENTITY AND IMAGINATION OF IMMIGRANT CHILDREN

Figure 4-1: Diego's sketch

originally lived. He wrote "Puerto Rico"— which represents my homeland; "El Salvador"—his birthplace; "Mexico"—from which most of the students emigrated; "Nigeria"—making reference to the one student in the larger class who came from Africa; "United States"—which is the place we all came to and our present location, which also could be interpreted as the ESL teacher's homeland. In his sketch, Diego created a common place location to visually interpret the literary text and his experiences, and he connected those to the present moment in the classroom. Past history and present reality were all embedded in the location he created to interpret the text. Furthermore, in his written description he established the difference between what constituted his personal connection ("My art reminds me when I crossed the border") and what he considered to be the meaning of the sketch ("My art means when Amanda crossed the border"), making reference to the main character in the literary text. Through a visual representation Diego added to the literature discussions, creating a common place location between text, personal past, and collective present in the classroom.

Common Place Location #3: Drama Structures

The third literary engagement we used to interpret the text was process drama (O'Neill 1995). Using elements of process drama structures helped us explore moments within the text and also move outside the text's boundaries to imagine the characters' lives in the future. First I present a description of the whole drama, followed by samples and descriptions of the students' work within the drama. The significance of this experience is grounded in the close reality between the make-believe world and the students' lives. The context of the drama worked as a common place location to bring personal beliefs, feelings, and cultural knowledge to the forefront. Furthermore, it also worked as a space in which to explore tensions and contested ideologies in the classroom.

Writing in role through character diaries The text of *My Diary from Here to There/Mi Diario de Aquí Hasta Allá* is written in a diary form. Therefore, "writing in role" became a powerful strategy to utilize throughout the reading. We began our drama with the moment after the father crossed the border to Los Angeles. The students assumed the role of one of the characters and wrote diary entries reflecting upon their feelings about moving to the United States. The following example is Ivonne's writing in role as Amanda.

Hola diario:
Sabes, hoy me siento mal y a la vez me siento triste porque dejo a mi mejor amiga y mi tierra donde nací. Yo y mi familia no sabemos cuando regresaremos. Y a la vez me siento alegre porque voy a conocer una nueva ciudad y nueva gente pero eso si nunca se me olvidara quien soy. Lo bueno es que no dejamos a ningún familiar.

Hi diary:
You know, today I feel bad and at the same time I feel sad because I am leaving my best friend and the country where I was born. Me and my family do not know when we will return. And at the same time I feel happy because I am going to meet a new city and new people but that is all right I will never forget who I am. The good thing is that we are not leaving any family member behind.

Similar to some of the ideas explored in the literature discussion, Ivonne shared the complex feelings embedded in moving to a new country. She felt sad not only because she left friends behind but also because she was leaving her native country. At the same time, she revealed an excitement toward the possibility of knowing a new city and people. Furthermore, through the character's voice, Ivonne reaffirmed a sense of cultural identity by stating "I will never forget who I am."

Interviewing the characters on their first day of school in the United States Pérez ends the book with Amanda writing her first diary entry in her new home in Los Angeles. This ending creates the possibility for students to imagine the characters' experiences in a new context. In a form of hotseat, two students volunteered to take on the roles of Amanda and her brother Raúl. The rest of the class met in small groups to generate some interesting questions to ask the characters. Once the questioning began, the drama structure was affected by a shift from creating and communicating meaning using Spanish to establishing a space in which to practice English language skills.

[Diego takes Raul's role, Ivonne takes Amanda's role and the other students are interviewers]
    FRANCISCO: ¿A donde naciste Amanda?
    TEACHER: Can you ask in English?
    FRANCISCO: Oh.
    TEACHER: What do you want to say?
    FRANCISCO: Where are you from?
[Silence]
IVONNE (AMANDA): Ciudad Juarez. I am from Ciudad Juarez.
    YOLANDA: ¿Tu soportas a tu hermano?
    TEACHER: Can you say it in English?
    YOLANDA: Es que no se como se dice.
    CARMEN: Do you get along with your brother?
    YOLANDA: Do you get along with your brother?
IVONNE (AMANDA): ¿Como se dice "hay veces"?
    CARMEN: Sometimes.
    IVONNE: Sometimes.

An interesting aspect of this particular moment in the drama was the shift from using Spanish as the main language for communication to English. The teacher's intentions of using the drama context to "practice" English language skills shifted the drama from a space to share ideas into a language practice space. The students' efforts changed from "Do I have a powerful question to ask?" to "How can I ask a question using the repertoire of English vocabulary I know?" This event could be analyzed from two perspectives. One perspective is that the students in the context of the drama were somehow "practicing" and exploring English in a "meaningful" context. The other perspective for analysis is that the imposition of using English within the drama broke down the creative and spontaneous nature of creating a meaningful "make-believe world" and it resulted as a form of silencing. Language negotiations between the real and the fictional were key to this drama event, and resurfaced again in other parts of the drama.

Tableaux: Amanda and Raúl's first day of school Following the interviews, small groups of students created frozen images of Amanda and/or Raúl in their classrooms the first day of school. Each group revealed its tableau, and the class interpreted the images. For example, one of the powerful images constructed by a group of girls represented the teacher standing up in the front of the class pointing with her hand to the chalkboard. At the same time a group of girls was represented in the back of the classroom looking at an open book and talking among themselves. The image represented the kind of support that English language learners provide each other in the classroom in order to make sense and understand the materials and curricular content in English within the classroom. What could have been perceived as "not paying attention" was a demonstration of the kind support systems children develop among themselves in order to navigate English monolingual approaches to teaching.

Writing in role: Diary after first day of class Following the *characters'* experiences on the first day of class, the drama continued as the characters went back to their houses and wrote in their diaries. The students explored diverse perspectives in their diaries (see Medina 2005 for a detailed discussion). The perspectives ranged from sharing very positive experiences, to writing about mixed feelings, to revealing negative comments related to the unknown and/or communication barriers. However, it was the social dynamics of making friends and relating to people that was present in all of the diaries. Jorge's diary in role is one example:

> Es la primera vez que voy a la escuela en California. Mis carnales Antonio y Luis escuchamos musica en ingles para aprender ingles.

> *This is the first time I go to the school in California. My buddies Antonio and Luis listen to music in English so we can learn English.*

Jorge shared the importance of friendships and relationships in schools. Interestingly, Jorge used the setting in the book (California) but used his real friends' names, Antonio and Luis, who were both participants in this study. He brought the context of the book and his life to the drama interpretation. Furthermore, similar to the networks of support represented by the girls in the tableaux, he established how his network of friends enjoyed listening to music so they could learn English.

Experts as newcomers to schools: Challenges and solutions In role, the students were informed that they were selected by the superintendent of the school district to develop a document (the original intention was to create a video) about the biggest challenges new immigrants face in schools and possible ways to overcome those challenges. The "experts," armed with chart paper and markers, brainstormed ideas and possible solutions to create a bilingual document. The following is a collection of excerpts from the larger dialogue we had while negotiating the creation of the document:

FRANCISCO: Hacer amigos
 Make friends.
YOLANDA: Con la tarea.
 With homework.
FRANCISCO: Explicando hasta que aprenda.
 Explain until they learn.
[negotiation among students to write down the phrase]
 IVONNE: Aquí hay una niña que se llama Flavia . . . me explica hasta que entendiendo.
 Here there is a girl named Flavia . . . she explains to me until I understand.
 DIEGO: Que no entiende inglés.
 That you don't understand English.
 IVONNE: Traducirles.
 Translate.
FRANCISCO: Cuando te ponen un trabajo en inglés que no entiendes es lo mas difícil.
 When they give you work in English that you don't understand is the most difficult.

DIEGO: Hablar con las maestras es bien difícil.
Talking to the teachers is very difficult.
YOLANDA: Porque si no lo entiendes . . . Busca una persona que hable español e inglés.
Because if you do not understand . . . find a person who speaks Spanish and English.
FRANCISCO: Le hubieras puesto maestra y aquí le hubieras puesto la "o" como maestro.
You should have put "maestra" [female teacher] and here put down an "o" like "maestro" [male teacher].
YOLANDA: Entender las palabras importantes.
Understand important words.
CARMEN: ¿Cuales son las palabras importantes?
What are the important words?
YOLANDA: ¿Puedo ir a la oficina? *Can I go to the office?*
DIEGO: Con rojo [making reference to the marker color]
With red.
FRANCISCO: Con verde. Verde, blanco, y rojo.
With green. Green, white, and red.
[Pause]
FRANCISCO: I can go to the office. My mother was here in the office.
YOLANDA: Can I go to the bathroom?
DIEGO: ¿Puedo ir al baño.
YOLANDA: I am hungry.
FRANCISCO: I can go drink the water.
YOLANDA: Can I get a drink of water?
FRANCISCO: Yo no se decirlo bien.
I do not know how to say it correctly.
DIEGO: Puedo ir a tomar agua.

There were various interesting aspects during this particular moment in the drama. The students as experts had a sense of "audience" for whom they were constructing this document and critically reflected on school as a location where multiple social and linguistic positions were negotiated. As in other moments in the drama, communication and social relationships were at the center of the challenges they faced as new immigrants in a new school. Homework, in-class work, and communication with teachers were perceived as the biggest challenges. The explorations of these challenges were embedded in their personal experiences in schools.

Rooted in their talk were other important identity and linguistic discourses that the students brought to this moment. First they talked about homework and communication with teachers. Within this talk Francisco brought an interesting gender perspective to the construction of the document. He pointed out that an "o" should be substituted for the "a" in the Spanish word "*maestra*" (which represents female teachers) to convey the idea that a barrier also exists in communicating with "*maestros*," the male teachers in the school. Furthermore, later on in the transcript Francisco suggested the use of red, green, and white for use in the document, thereby incorporating the colors of the Mexican flag. In this situated moment the students reflected and created a common place location where drama and personal identity intersected, creating many layers between reality and fiction.

Within the multiple forms of communication that the students navigated in schools, they also established a hierarchy of what constituted important "phrases." In that situated moment the students did an interesting shift on linguistic resources. They shifted to a more hybrid use of English and Spanish as they tried to summarize and convey the meaning of phrases such as: "Can I go to the office?" "Can I go to the bathroom?" "I am hungry." It is important to signal that most of these phrases are related to "asking for permission" to do something. Their phrases are embedded in an awareness of power relations within the school, and learning those relations are a priority in order to succeed in school.

CONCLUSIONS

This drama structure provided a powerful context to explore aspects of the students' social realities that could be related to critical literacies. Similar to forms of Latina/o theatre/drama that explore participants' social realities (Boal 1979; Broyles-Gonzáles 1994; Medina and Campano in press), the participants were challenged to investigate possibilities in real-life situations close to their life experiences as recent immigrants. The drama worked as a common place location where the students analyzed the characters and their social realities, grounded in their personal experiences and emotions.

The multiple drama examples I shared in this chapter demonstrate how in this drama, the students used the context of the story and each student's personal voice to interpret a moment in a character's life. These interpretations were framed in relationship to the students' experiences coming to a new country. As I looked across the drama, I was particularly fascinated by the representation of friendships and relationships among the students to develop support networks. In the tableaux, writing in role, and as experts, the students communicated the critical role they play in each other's lives in schools to negotiate language, knowledge, and identity. Furthermore, they also explored the tensions and challenges of language imposition and power that children whose first language is other than English face in their schooling experiences. In my opinion, the students created common place locations where imagination and reality were blurred.

One of the significant aspects of the process I described was the opportunity to see how the children designed and redesigned representations of meaning around texts and experiences (The New London Group 2000) through talk, visual arts, and drama. We created various common place locations for literary interpretation where the students mediated knowledge through multiple literacies:

1. *linguistic and cultural literacy*, using the students' language and cultural resources across sign systems but also negotiating related, larger ideological tensions
2. *talk and dialogue*, allowing students to make sense and acquire new perspectives on a "common" experience with a literary text
3. *visual literacy*, providing an opportunity to interpret culture and their histories in new ways in the present moment through visual images
4. *drama literacy*, seen in the embodiment of characters and situations that represent the larger experiences of the students as recent immigrants and border crossers.

The combination of sign systems provided diverse ways to make meaning and represent knowledge. Furthermore, each of these representations became a common place location to interpret emotional, geographical, physical, and social aspects of the students' past and present identities as recent immigrants.

REFERENCES

Anzaldúa, Gloria. 1987. *Borderlands/La Frontera: The New Mestiza*. California: Aunt Lute Books.

Berghoff, Beth, Kathy Egawa, Jerome Harste, and Barry Hoonan. 2000. *Beyond Reading and Writing: Inquiry, Curriculum and Multiple Ways of Knowing*. Illinois: NCTE.

Boal, Augusto. 1979. *Theatre of the Oppressed*. Trans. C. A. and M. Leal McBride. New York: Theatre Communications Group. Original work published 1974 by Urizen Books.

Broyles-Gonzáles, Yolanda. 1994. *El Teatro Campesino*. Texas: University of Texas Press.

Calderón, Hector, and José David Saldívar, eds. 1991. *Criticism in the Borderlands: Studies on Chicano Literature, Culture and Ideology*. Durham, North Carolina: Duke University Press.

Enciso, Patricia, and Brian Edmiston. 1997. "Drama and Response to Literature: Reading the Text and Re-reading the Truth." In *Reader Response in Elementary Classroom: Quest and Discovery*, edited by Nicholas Karolides, 69–94. New Jersey: Lawrence Erlbaum.

Jewitt, Carey, Gunther Kress, Jon Ogborn, and Charalampos Tsatsarelis. 2001. "Exploring Learning Through Visual, Actional and Linguistic Communication: The Multimodal Environment of a Science Classroom." *Educational Review* 53(1): 5–14.

Medina, Carmen. 2004. "Drama Wor(l)ds: Explorations of Latina/o Realistic Fiction Through Drama." *Language Arts* 81(4): 10–20.

Medina, Carmen. (2005). "Discourse and Ideology in Writing in Role: Critical Discourse Analysis as Tool for Interpretation." *Youth Theatre Journal* 19:102–114.

Medina, Carmen, and Gerald Campano. (in press). "Performing identities through drama and teatro practices in multilingual classrooms." *Language Arts*.

New London Group. 2000. "Multiliteracies: Literacy Learning and the Design of Social Futures." In *Multiliteracies: Literacy Learning and the Design of Social Futures*, edited by B. Cope and M. Kalantzis, 9–37. London: Routledge.

O'Neill, Cecily. 1995. *Drama Worlds: A Framework for Process Drama*. New Hampshire: Heinemann.

Pérez, Amada Irma. 2002. *My Diary from Here to There / Mi Diario de Aquí Hasta Allá*. Illustrated by M. C. Gonzalez. California: Children's Books Press.

Rogers, Theresa, and Cecily O'Neill. 1993. "Creating Multiple Worlds: Drama, Language and Literary Response." In *Exploring Texts: The Role of Discussion and Writing in the Teaching and Learning of Literature*, edited by G. Newel and R. K. Durst, 69–89. Massachusetts: Christopher-Gordon Publishers.

Rosenblatt, Louise. 1978. *The Reader, The Text, The Poem. The Transactional Theory of the Literary Work*. Illinois: Southern Illinois University Press.

Short, Kathy, Jerome Harste, and Carolyn Burke. 1996. *Creating Classrooms for Authors and Inquirers*. New Hampshire: Heinemann.

Siegel, Marjorie. 1995. "More Than Words: The Generative Power of Transmediation for Learning." *Canadian Journal of Education* 20(4): 455–475.

Sumara, Dennis. 1996. *Private Readings in Public: Schooling the Literary Imagination*. New York: Peter Lang.

_____. 2001. "Learning to Create Insight: Literary Engagements as Purposeful Pedagogy." *Changing English* 8(2): 165–175.

_____. 2002. *Why Reading Literature Still Matters: Imagination, Interpretation and Insight*. New Jersey: Lawrence Erlbaum.

5
"I'm a lot like her": Entering the World of *Others* Through Process Drama

Karen S. Kelley

Seven girls sat huddled in *their* spot, reading a chapter from *The Watsons Go to Birmingham—1963* (Curtis 1995). When I leaned down to join the group, I discovered that the girls were orally revising the chapter so that it was told from a completely different character's point of view. Intrigued, I stayed with the group and asked if I could try it. It was HARD!—yet the girls did it with seeming ease. They possessed a motivation that I apparently lacked. To gain insight into their motivation, I asked Jenny (all student names are pseudonyms) why they were making the changes. She replied, "because our character, Joetta, the princess of the family, is the most important character. We want to be the center of attention" (Field notes, February 25). This group of girls in Toni Lazzaro's intermediate, multiage class (third, fourth, and fifth grades) engaged in a five-week process drama unit based upon *The Watsons Go to Birmingham—1963*. Toni, the classroom teacher, and I, the assistant principal, conceived this project first as an investigation into the impact of process drama on reading comprehension. We were also concerned about increasing the students' awareness of the relationships within the fictional family of the Watsons and the racial tensions existing in Alabama in 1963. However, as I observed the Joetta character group intentionally and spontaneously orally revising the text so it would be told from their character's point of view, I realized we were experiencing something much more. The members of this group of white and Latina girls from rural, central Florida came together to form the Joetta character group and connected with Joetta (an African American character in the story) in ways that crossed racial lines. The talk, the writing, the reading, and performances of the Joetta character are the focus of this chapter.

BRINGING THE WORLD OF THE WATSONS ALIVE

Three key concepts, discussed by O'Neill (1995), gave this particular process drama unit form: pre-text, structural devices, and the unique role of the teacher. Pre-texts, in this case *The Watsons Go to Birmingham—1963*, allow a process drama event to begin to take shape. The selection of this pre-text provided a firm base from which the imagined world proceeded. *The Watsons Go to Birmingham—1963* had immediate implications for further action, including speaking, writing, and participating in process drama devices, because two themes—family relationships and racial tensions—run throughout the text. The story blends the fictional account of the Watsons, an African American family, with the factual events of the turbulent summer of 1963 in Birmingham, Alabama. Kenny, the younger brother and narrator, tells of hilarious episodes involving Daniel, the father; Wilona, the mother; Byron, eldest brother; and Joetta, the youngest sibling and only daughter, that reveal conflict within the family. The family members' reactions to Byron's juvenile delinquent tendencies allow the reader to understand the personalities of these five characters. The family travels to Birmingham to make good on a threat to send Byron to the Deep South to spend the summer with his strict grandmother, and they find themselves in the middle of the burning of the Sixteenth Avenue Baptist Church with four little girls inside. The text served as the backdrop against which the process drama devices proceeded.

The success of any process drama experience relies not only on careful selection of a pre-text but also on the selection of the mode of activity for each episode. Modes of activity are referred to as structural devices and include "watching, inquiry, games and contests, appearances, roles within roles, public and private dimensions, and rituals" (O'Neill 1995, 131). For our purposes, we identified two structural devices that put our students in positions to enter the imagined world of the Watson family in order to deal with both of the prevalent themes in the book. First, we explored family relationships by formulating an inquiry in the form of a trial. Byron was placed on trial for his constant antics, and all other family members were called to the stand to testify. Next, we explored reactions to the racial tensions brought up in the second half of the book as we facilitated a ritual in the form of a family dinner. Neither of these process drama events occurred in the text; rather, we entered the world of the Watson family through these structural devices. We created dramatic moments beginning with a pre-text that propelled the action forward through the work of the teacher(s), in and out of role.

A teacher in role is able to model appropriate behaviors and becomes a part of the imagined world (O'Neill 1995). "The role presented by the teacher is available to be 'read' publicly, and, like spectators at a play, the participants are entangled in a web of contemplation, speculation, and anticipation" (O'Neill 1995, 61). Our challenge in this conception of the teacher in role came when we considered the issue of control. During the trial, I played the role of a judge, Toni played the role of prosecuting attorney, and one other teacher, Dawn, played the defense attorney. Thus we held three powerful roles in the drama. We met prior to the trial to outline a general order to the proceedings; however, the actual trial proceeded without a script for the teachers or the students. The drama unfolded in response to the students' participation. During the family dinner, I was the only teacher in role. As the teacher in role, I assumed the role of Grandma Sands at the Watsons' dinner table. My role in this drama was less involved than the trial because the students responded to each other at the table, much like a family dinner would proceed. The teacher in role in a process drama device is not to give a display of acting or to gain control; rather, it is one of participation in cooperation with the participants (O'Neill 1995).

GROUPING FOR LEARNING IN THE DRAMA CONTEXT

Students were organized into five groups, one for each of the main characters. The academic goals of comprehending the text, relating to the family relationships in the text, and understanding the racial tensions of 1963, along with the highly social nature of the classroom activities and structural devices, led us to consider several factors when forming the groups.

First, we viewed learning from a sociocultural perspective, and therefore, as a social enterprise (Vygotsky 1986). High-performing cooperative learning groups are defined as groups in which "students are given two responsibilities: to maximize their own learning and to maximize the learning of all other group members" (Johnson and Johnson 1999, 24). Therefore, we wanted the group members to exhibit the highest level of commitment to each other.

Second, the social status of group members impacts the end result of the group thinking: ideas from students with higher social status are more likely to be valued, while ideas from students with lower social status are likely to be ignored, rejected, or absent (Matthews and Kesner 2003). "The nature and quality of the relationships between the participants in a group also contribute to the degree to which the interactions among the participants are successful" (Matthews and Kesner 2003, 230). Therefore, if the social relationships of participants are significant to the success of the group, those relationships should be considered when forming the groupings.

Third, academic goals must be a factor in forming groups for collaborative literacy events. For the purposes of this dramatic exploration, we considered our academic and social goals to form groups based upon existing social relationships.

As the basis for her decisions in forming groups, Toni conducted interviews with each of the twenty-seven students in her language arts classroom. The interviews allowed Toni to determine the students' interests outside of school, friendships, common means of transportation to and from school, and past classroom experiences. An intricate web of relationships resulted. Together, Toni and I formed groups around the commonalities found in these interviews. For example, the group that assumed the role of Joetta was linked together by (1) being in the same team/classroom for several years and (2) participating in outside interests such as cheerleading and chorus. Each character group ranged in size from five to seven students. The Joetta character group was composed of seven girls, six white and one Latina. We hoped to lessen the impact that social status had on participation in the process drama events by forming groups around natural social connections. We were not naive enough to think we would eliminate the social factors at work during such activity, merely lessen their influence on these highly social events.

THE WATSONS GO TO BIRMINGHAM—THE INSTRUCTIONAL PLAN

The five-week unit included several classroom instructional strategies and structural devices (see Figure 5–1). The students participated in a

	Classroom Activities	Structural Devices
Week One	• lessons from WebQuest • reading of chapters 1–5 • character group discussions and journal entries • modeling of journal entries in role	
Week Two	• lessons from WebQuest • reading of chapters 6–8 • character group discussions and journal entries • introduction of Byron's impending trial	
Week Three	• lessons from WebQuest • reading of chapters 9–10 • character group discussions and journal entries	• Byron's trial
Week Four	• lessons from WebQuest • reading of chapters 11–14 • character group discussions and journal entries	
Week Five	• lessons from WebQuest • reading of chapter 15 & Epilogue • character group discussions and journal entries • Reading Counts quiz on *The Watsons Go to Birmingham—1963*	• family dinner
2 weeks later	• written summary of *The Watsons Go to Birmingham—1963*	

Figure 5-1: Outline of classroom activities and structural devices

WebQuest (Lazzaro 2003) developed by Toni in order to activate prior knowledge and build foundational knowledge about 1963. A WebQuest is an inquiry-oriented set of activities in which most or all of the information used by the students is located on the Web (Dodge 1995). Throughout the project, students read chapters from the book individually, in small groups, and by listening on tape. Following each chapter, the character groups discussed the chapter from their character's point of view and responded to the events in role in a simulated journal. In simulated journals, children assume the identity of another person in real life or of a character in a book and write from that person's viewpoint (Tompkins 2004). In this case, the simulated journals became a place for students responding in role to record thoughts, feelings, and reactions.

From Lena's journal, writing in role as Joetta

Dear Diary,
Today my smarty pants brother read in front of Byron and Buphead's sixth grade class. Everyone (except the teacher) made fun of Kenny. I feel kind of bad for him, though. Only two good things happened to Kenny today. 1. Byron fixed his lazy eye, And 2. there was a new kid on the bus and everyone made fun of him instead of Kenny. I feel bad for the new kid and wish that he wasn't made fun of but I also wish that Kenny wasn't made fun of either. Kenny called him his savior but I don't think he notices that this kid is going to get made fun of just the same as he was. Just think how bad Kenny felt, now this kid is going to feel just as bad.
Sincerely,
Joetta

Through her writing, Lena entered Joetta's world and captured the tone and emotion of the text (e.g., "my smarty pants brother"). She carried Joetta's voice into her response and went beyond the text to explore Joetta's possible emotions during Kenny's bus incident. Even though she was responding to an early chapter in the text, Lena's familiarity with Joetta is evident in the empathy she demonstrated toward the new boy on the bus (e.g., now the kid is going to feel just as bad).

Similarly, Jenny entered Joetta's world and applied her own version of Joetta's voice in her journal entry for a later chapter.

Dear Journal,
We are back from Birmingham. I'm glad. The weird thing is Kenny keeps disappearing off somewhere. I wish I knew where he was going. The other day he was in the bathroom crying. Nobody tells me anything anymore. Maybe it's because I'm little. When

Kenny is out he would play with me very little. It's time for dinner. Bye.

Joetta, aka Princess of not knowing anything.

Jenny's line of thinking is her own, but it is based upon her knowledge of Joetta and her world. Jenny's response goes beyond a low-level connection and builds in an emotional understanding of her character. The simulated journals provided a space for the Joetta character group to connect with their character and enter another's world. These types of connections set the stage for the Joetta character group's participation in both process drama devices that were a part of the instructional plan for this unit.

The First Drama Event: Byron's Trial

On the day of the trial, the room was arranged to imitate a courtroom. I sat before the audience of witnesses preparing to act as judge, with the two attorneys (teachers) facing me. All five students who were acting as the defendant, Byron Watson, sat next to the defense counsel, Dawn. The other character groups, for Kenny, Joetta, Wilona, and Daniel Watson, sat as witnesses in the audience behind the two attorneys. The bailiff sat to the right of the judge, prepared to swear in all witnesses, who would sit to the left of the judge facing out toward the audience. As the Kenny character group was sworn in, the Joetta character group squealed with distress at the pending doom of their brother. Each member of the Joetta group held a Kleenex in her hand to dab away her tears as the trial proceeded. The Joetta group became particularly distressed as the Wilona character group, the mother, testified to the many devious incidents in Byron's past that led to this trial. At one point, the judge issued a stern warning to the Joetta group members, who were weeping above the testimony of the Wilona character group: "Prosecution, one moment please. Joettas, if you cannot remain quiet and orderly, I'm afraid I'll have to ask you to leave the courtroom immediately" (Trial transcript, April 4). The Joetta group quieted their crying, but continued to use their Kleenex to dab their wet, tear-filled eyes.

The Joetta group's time on the stand was filled with tension. On one hand, the Joettas decided prior to the trial that they did not support Byron being sent away. On the other hand, when faced with having to testify regarding the facts of Byron's behavior, they had to tell the truth. The tension between their personal feelings and telling the truth on the stand manifested itself in shy looks among the group members and long hesitations before giving each potentially incriminating answer. They even tried to qualify their answers to make their responses seem more favorable toward Byron, their brother:

TONI (prosecuting attorney): Is it a fact that your brother, the juvenile, tried to burn down your house?
JOETTA: (all looking at one another) yes, no, yes, no, no
TONI: He tried to burn down your house with your pets in it?
JOETTA: No.
TONI: Tell us about that incident.
JOETTA: (One member dabbing eyes with Kleenex, long pause.) He lit the match, but then he flushed them down the toilet. He needed fire for his flamethrower of death and then flushed it.
TONI: Don't you think your brother should be punished for his bad behavior?
JOETTA: (Some heads shaking yes, others no.) He has been punished already by mom. (Trial transcript, April 4)

Although the students worked together to form the Joetta character, two members did not provide verbal responses during the trial. Students who do not participate verbally during a process drama event may very well participate internally. Both of these students provided evidence of their engagement in the events of the trial in their letters composed after the trial. Becky, writing as Joetta, drew upon her familiarity with her character when she wrote to Judge Kelley.

Dear Honorable Judge Kelley,
You should not take my brother Byron to Juvinile Deliquent Center, because he is my big brother, and who is going to stick up for me if he leaves. Prosecutor—Ms. Lazarro was wrong. She wants to take Byron to that place that has all the Juvinile Deliquent Kids. Defense—Mrs. Gwuynn [defense attorney] was accurate, he was doing all this terrible mess because he was missunder stood. Court today was scarey. But if he went we won't get to see him for a very lengthy time. punishment for Byron is to never leave the house except going to school and studing.
Sincerly,
Joetta Watson

In her letter, Becky summarized the events of the trial while taking sides with the defense attorney. Yet, she did not communicate these thoughts during the trial. Writing the letter to Judge Kelley was the outlet through which Becky processed the information in the text and the events of the trial in order to support her opinion regarding Byron's future. Similarly, Beth, writing as Joetta, supported Byron and wanted him to remain with her family.

> Dear Honorable Judge Kelley
> I really do not want you to send Byron to juvie cause theen I will not have anybody to keep me warm or to keep me from getting hurt from some old ugly bully. When Kenny gets older and I get older and Byron is still in juvie Kenny probly will not take care of me. I will miss Byron so much and I really want hime to stay.

Both Becky and Beth synthesized, analyzed, and evaluated the characters' plights during and after the trial. Both Beth and Becky saw the long-term ramifications of the judge's decision, however, they did not share their opinion verbally during the trial. The opportunity to write a letter to the judge gave both students the venue to reveal their thinking indicating that both had actively participated during the trial. While the Joetta character group noted Byron's faults, the group valued their family member and realized that without him their family unit would not be whole. They also recognized that Byron's absence would greatly impact Joetta's (their) personal safety.

The day after the trial, I returned to hand down the ruling in Byron's case. After considering the testimony and the written input from each witness, I found Byron guilty of being a juvenile delinquent and sentenced him to travel to Grandma Sands' home in Birmingham, Alabama—the same outcome followed in the book. By allowing the trial to parallel the book, I felt the outcome would support their remaining reading. When I handed down my decision, some character groups yelled a controlled "yes" (e.g., the Joetta character group) while other character groups tried to protest (e.g., the Wilona character group) (Field notes, April 5). The reaction from the character groups was mixed, but they followed the same emotional tendencies exhibited during the trial.

The Second Drama Event: The Watson Family Dinner

At the conclusion of the book, individual students from each character group met in a family group for a Sunday dinner. We conducted five family dinners to allow each student a chance to participate individually in character. As was true for Byron's trial, the family dinner did not actually occur in the book. Instead, it was a structural device categorized as a ritual (O'Neill 1995). Toni and I created a family setting at the dinner table in the media center. To add to the feel of this ritual and draw students into the imaginary world of a family dinner in the Watson household, we provided a meal of some small snacks and a drink. Our goal for the family dinner conversation was to give the students an opportunity "in character" to debrief the dramatic real-world events the family experienced while in Birmingham. During the family dinner, I worked in role as Grandma Sands to establish the context for the drama. I began each family dinner by explaining my presence in Flint, Michigan. "I rushed to Michigan to be sure my precious family was okay. You [the Watson family] left Birmingham so quickly I was worried and had to know what you thought about what happened there" (Family dinner transcripts May 5). During the dinner, I asked probing questions about the social conditions in Birmingham and specifically about the bombing that occurred, prompting the family's quick retreat home to Michigan. In a true family dinner fashion, other family members interrupted conversations, disagreements among family members were exposed, and in some cases, minds were changed about conclusions of the events in Birmingham:

GRANDMA SANDS: Daniel, why did you insist on bringing your family back to Birmingham so quickly?
DANIEL: I was afraid one of us was going to get hurt.
GRANDMA SANDS: Joetta, what do you think your dad is talking about?
JOETTA: Well, the whites and blacks weren't getting . . .
DANIEL: (interrupting) That's right, the whites and blacks. Whites aren't very fond of us blacks, but we aren't very fond of them either.
GRANDMA SANDS: Well, I've got to tell you how sorry I am that I even suggested that you come to Birmingham. When Wilona called to tell me about the problems with you (points at Byron), we came up with the plan to bring you down to Birmingham; my neighborhood was as safe as could be. I am so sorry about bringing you down there.
BYRON: Sorry mom.
WILONA: Sorry, what for?
BYRON: For, um, being so bad that all of us had to go down there. My baby sister almost got killed.
GRANDMA SANDS: Ain't that something? He just apologized for putting your lives in danger.

DANIEL: I really appreciate it, but we didn't know until a few days after we got there, so it's not all of his fault (patting Byron's shoulder as he talks)

JOETTA: I accept his apology. I didn't want him to go in the first place!

(Family dinner May 5)

This family group responded to the danger in Birmingham by drawing upon events that occurred throughout the text and during the trial. Joetta drew upon her participation in the trial when she stated that she hadn't wanted Byron to be sent away. Byron's apology was also something that did not happen in the text; however, it reveals a level of understanding of the character that developed over the course of the unit. During a different family dinner, another Joetta offered opinions based upon her experiences with the WebQuest and drew upon connections she made between the text and other classroom experiences.

JOETTA: I don't think Birmingham would be such a good idea with the whole church thing.

GRANDMA SANDS: Out of the mouths of babes. The youngest one in the family is the only one who realizes how serious the situation is. Daniel and Wilona, do you have anything to say about some of your family wanting to move to Birmingham?

WILONA: Well, they have friends in Flint and in Alabama, well, there's . . .

DANIEL: (interrupting) It's dangerous down there. I just don't like the idea.

GRANDMA SANDS: (interrupting) Oh, that was just a one-time thing. It's all right.

BYRON: You think it's the same way as when you were growing up. We see it different, the bombing, Kenny almost drowning.

JOETTA: You're talking to Grandma that way? Sassing. Ummmm . . .

BYRON: I'm talking to mama.

GRANDMA SANDS: Such disrespect. I thought you'd changed, Byron?

WILONA: Do I need to get some more matches? (The eyes of every family member widened with the mention of matches, and a long silence followed.)

GRANDMA SANDS: Daniel and Wilona, knowing what you know about Birmingham, would you want to raise your children there?

WILONA: Well, no. They could die of heat flashes. They have black crusades. I don't really like that too much. We might get into danger down there. We already did. In Flint, the kids have their friends.

BYRON: But living in Birmingham might not be too bad because where we live at it is too cold. (Wilona looks as Byron inquisitively.) All those clothes you put on Kenny and Joetta, that's a shame.

JOETTA: We fit in better in Flint.

KENNY: I think Birmingham because Grandma Sands spoils us.

JOETTA: If you were going to spoil us, you could put five air conditioners in our rooms.

GRANDMA SANDS: Oh, you guys are tougher than that.

JOETTA: You know this whole thing was white people trying kill all us in that church.

GRANDMA SANDS: And that is some place you'd want to raise these children?

DANIEL: No.

WILONA: I think we are fine in Flint. I'm not proud of my decision to take everyone to Birmingham.

KENNY: Yeah, I guess we need to stay here. (Family dinner May 5)

In the end, Kenny changed his mind about wanting to live in Birmingham. Just as in the simulated journals, the opinions captured in these transcripts are evidence that the students entered the world of the Watsons and came to know their characters. The comments made by Joetta and other family members are evidence of extensions made beyond the text based upon knowledge of the characters.

At the conclusion of each family dinner, I asked the family if they would ever agree to return to Birmingham to see me, Grandma Sands, again. Four of the five groups agreed to see Grandma Sands again despite the social situations that existed there. The one family group that did not agree felt it was just too dangerous and that Byron had definitely learned his lesson. To appease Grandma Sands, they invited her to visit them again in Michigan.

CREATING SPACES TO CONNECT WITH CHARACTERS

Entering the world of the Watson family came easily for the Joetta character group. The process drama devices, combined with the simulated journals, created spaces in which the girls made text-to-self connections that helped them make sense of difficult issues in the text (Keene and Zimmermann 1997). The act of making text-to-self connections emphasizes the role of the reader in making intertextual links (Bloome and Egan Robertson 1993). From a semiotic perspective, intertextuality, or the juxtaposition of different texts, includes the idea of text not only as literary texts, but also the text of one's own life (Kristeva 1980). In the following interview excerpts, the Joetta characters revealed their use of the texts of their lives to relate with Joetta, making text-to-self connections that crossed racial boundaries.

>   LENA: "As we started to know each other a lot of us had things in common with each other and with Joetta."
>   HANNAH: "I liked being Joetta. That is kind of my part in real life. I am the little sister to two older brothers. My older brother is kind of the troublemaker."
>   JENNY: "I wish I would have been Byron because I'm more like Byron because I get in trouble sometimes by my mom and Joetta did not."
>   [Lena asked me to read her journal today. She commented that this family was just like her family and Heather's family. She emphasized that she was not a princess like Joetta, but she, Hannah, and Rachel are both the youngest girl in their family, just like Joetta." (Field notes February 25, 2003)]

Despite the fact that the family dinner, the WebQuest, the simulated journal, and character group discussions addressed the extreme racial conditions that existed in Birmingham in 1963, those racial concerns are absent from the text-to-self connections made in the Joetta character group. Towell, Schulz, and Demetrulias (1997) suggest that students identify with characters in children's books based on plots and similar interests rather than relating to ethnicity. The case of Lena and Hannah specifically confirms the proposition that text-to-self connections are made without reference to ethnicity. They related to Joetta as the youngest sibling and only sister in a family with two older brothers. They related to Joetta as the princess of the family.

Role-driven writing (Booth 1998) contributed to the creation of a space in which students could connect with characters and enter the world of *others*. Writing in role in simulated journals and acting in role during the two process drama structural devices allowed students to enter a "sphere of attitudes and feeling" (Booth 1998, 73). The frequency with which the Joetta character group expressed feelings beyond the level of a basic retelling is evidenced in the degree to which the Joetta character group entered the sphere of attitudes and feelings surrounding the Watson family in their journals.

From Kathy's journal

Da Da Da Hear comes lipless wonder to save the day. I thought I was going to pee my pants when my brother or should we say lipless wonder got his little lips got stuck on the winda. All us could not help but laughing that big bad Byron was stuck to the big brown turde [family car].

From Lena's journal

Today was the scariest day of my life because Byron almost burned. I just couldn't help crying and blowing the matches that momma lit. Byron was playing with fire again so mommy lit a match and stuck it real, real close to Byron's finger and he was screaming and crying like a little kindergardener. He was crying just as bad as I was! Boy was he scared and finally mommy gave up because I was extremely scared, too! Now I'm even kind of scared of momma and I think that Byron and Kenny are too!

Extremely Scared,
Joetta

From Becky's journal

Lord oh Lord oh Lord. Thank God or an angle like Kenny saved me from going to church. there was a bomb explosion, also I feel terribly sorry for those 4 little girls that died. Kenny is a life saver.

Sincerely,
Joetta

The social nature of these process drama events and the intentional grouping strategies we used during this collaborative literacy project (Matthews and Kesner 2003) did impact the connections the Joetta character group made.

LENA: "Sometimes we couldn't find a certain part. So, we looked and discussed a lot of things together to help us understand it more." (Interview May 28)

BECKY: Working with my group "helped because you knew these people and you knew you could discuss it with them all the stuff you have learned and help refresh their brains." (Interview May 28)

JENNY: "I know them (the girls in my group) because we were all in the same class and I knew them for years. It helped because when you know someone then it is a lot better than if you don't know anyone and they are trying to explain something to you."

RACHEL: [It was a good thing to be in a group with people I had a connection to]

"because you know them better and you can express yourself more and say about what you think and not have worry about what they think." (Interviews May 28)

Our purpose when intentionally grouping students to participate in the collaborative literacy events was to lessen the impact of social status within the group on the degree to which students participated in the process drama devices and other classroom activities. The comments from the Joetta character group indicate that the grouping did impact their participation, thus allowing them to fully enter the world of the Watsons.

FINAL THOUGHTS

The two-tiered instructional goals that Toni and I set out to accomplish blinded us to the potential of process drama as a point of connection with characters across racial lines. Our goal to improve reading comprehension (tier one) and our goal to increase awareness of larger societal issues (tier two), while noble, missed the mark. The Joetta group showed us that "process drama gives us the ability to wear other people's shoes and see the world from a different point of view" (O'Mara 2002, 30).

Lena, one of the white members of the Joetta character group, commented in her final interview, "I like being Joetta. I'm a lot like her. The Watson family is just like my family. I have two older brothers and I am the youngest and I am the girl. Then I have a mom and a dad who, both of them are a little strange, just like the Watsons. Now that I have read this book, now I call my family the weird Watsons just like in the book" (Interview, May 28). Lena's connections with Joetta, like those of her group, showed that she had entered the world of the Watsons but had not connected with the racial references. While "we all notice color in just about every situation we are in" (Kivel 2002, 13), Lena's affective and physical involvement drew her into the fictional world of the Watsons, where she could engage with the moral life being explored within it and come to know Joetta as a young girl, rather than as an African American (Winston 1999). Lena's memories of this character were not shaped by issues of color. In a moment of honesty, I must confess that Lena's connection, and those of all of her group members that did not mention issues of color, excited me. I saw this group coming to know Joetta as a girl—just a girl; however, noticing color is the only way to counteract the negative effect that racism has on people (Kivel 2002). Had this group truly entered the world of *others*? Had they noticed the racial issues that Joetta faced throughout the text and come to fully understand what it was to be Joetta during 1963 in Birmingham, Alabama? I want to believe that they did, but am left wondering.

By entering the world of the Watsons through the eyes of Joetta, a character with whom they easily identified, the Joetta character group was connecting with a character with whom they shared experiences and traits. Perhaps the Joettas easily adopted a point of view they had already identified with or personally experienced, thus limiting their potential for understanding (Edmiston and Wilhelm, 1998). We initially believed that issues of race might impact the connections the group would make. The converse occurred: The group connected with Joetta in many ways but did not look past the commonalities to explore the more difficult issues of race that Joetta faced in the text. It is not only in the realization of the connections between their own lives and the lives of *others* that complex understandings develop (Edmiston and Wilhelm 1998), but also in noticing and valuing the differences between their lives and the lives of *others*. There is no doubt that facilitating the type of work in which students enter the world of *others* is difficult, but it is definitely worthwhile.

REFERENCES

Bloome, David, and Ann Egan-Robertson. 1993. "The Social Construction of Intertextuality in Classroom Reading and Writing Lessons." *Reading Research Quarterly* 28 (October/November): 305–333.

Booth, David. 1998. "Language Power Through Working in Role." In *Educational Drama and Language Arts: What Research Shows*, edited by B. J. Wagner, 57–76. Portsmouth, NH: Heinemann.

REFERENCES

Curtis, Christopher Paul. 1995. *The Watsons Go to Birmingham—1963*. New York: Bantam Doubleday Dell Publishing Group, Inc.

Dodge, Bernie. 1995. "WebQuests: A Technique for Internet-Based Learning." *Distance Educator* 1 (2): 10–13.

Edmiston, Brian, and Jeffery Wilhelm. 1998. "Repositioning Views/Reviewing Positions: Forming Complex Understandings in Dialogue." In *Educational Drama and Language Arts: What Research Shows*, edited by B. J. Wagner, 90–117. Portsmouth, NH: Heinemann.

Johnson, David W., and Roger T. Johnson. 1999. "What Makes Cooperative Learning Work." In *JALT Applied Materials: Cooperative Learning*, edited by D. Kluge, S. McGuire, D. Johnson, and R. Johnson. Tokyo: Japan Association for Language Teaching. (ED 437 841)

Keene, Emily Oliver, and Susan Zimmermann. 1997. *Mosaic of Thought: Teaching Comprehension in a Reader's Workshop*. Portsmouth, NH: Heinemann.

Kivel, Paul. 2002. *Uprooting Racism: How White People Can Work for Racial Justice*. Gabriola Island, Canada: New Society Publishers.

Kristeva, Julia. 1980. "The Bounded Text." In *Desire in Language: A Semiotic Approach to Literature and Art*, edited by L. S. Roudiez. New York: Columbia University Press.

Lazzaro, Toni. 2003. "The Watsons Go to Birmingham, 1963. A WebQuest." http://cenes.pasco.k12.fl.us/homepage/teams/Trailblazers/Watson.htm (accessed July 23, 2004).

Matthews, Mona W., and John Kesner. 2003. "Children Learning with Peers: The Confluence of Peer Status and Literacy Competence Within Small-Group Literacy Events." *Reading Research Quarterly* 38 (2): 208–234.

O'Mara, Joanne. 2002. "Understanding the Complexity of Social Issues Through Process Drama." *Talking Points* 14(1): 27–30.

O'Neill, Cecily. 1995. *Drama Worlds: A Framework for Process Drama*. Portsmouth, NH: Heinemann.

Tompkins, Gail E. 2004. *Teaching Writing: Balancing Process and Product*, 4th ed. Columbus, OH: Pearson Merrill Prentice Hall.

Towell, Janet H., Armin Schultz, and Diana Mayer Demetrulias. 1997. *Does Ethnicity Really Matter in Literature for Young Children?* ERIC Clearinghouse. (ERIC Document Reproduction Service No. ED412571)

Winston, Joe. 1999. "Theorizing Drama as Moral Education." *Journal of Moral Education* 28(4): 459–471.

Vygotsky, Lev S. 1986. *Thought and Language*. Cambridge, MA: MIT Press.

6

Full Circling: How Visual Literacy, Narrative Texts, and Students' Imaginations Turned Urban Fifth-Graders into Architects of History

Trisha Wies Long

Imagine a young black boy[1] walking away in a beat-up section of a downtown street. It is a dismal day and the street is virtually deserted except for stray cars parked here and there. It's hard to tell whether there are people in the cars or not. The boy has on a raincoat but no shoes, and he's wearing a cap of indeterminate origins on his head. Although the street is desolate, it's crowded with the visages of the town's worn and weary effects. There's a handmade bench on the boy's right flanking *City Beauty Salon*, *"walk-ins served,"* and a number of *Public Telephone* signs hang high over his head. Further down the street we see a sign that says *Shoe-Shine Parlor*, followed by *Jean's Beauty Shop*. The grass on the ground—what's left of it—looks parched and dry, so we wonder why this boy is expecting rain. It is 1964 in Hattiesburg, Mississippi—*Freedom Summer*.

But here in twenty-first-century Midwest, a class of urban fifth-graders and I commence to "read" and "interpret" this Herbert Randall (1964) photograph as we begin a process of "full circling" (see Figure 6–1).[2]

---

[1] For the purposes of this article, which deals with the civil rights movement in the 1960s, the words "black" and "African American" will be used interchangeably.
[2] Randall, Herbert. Mobile Street Looking South. Hattiesburg, Mississippi, 1964. This photograph is Part of M351 Randall (Herbert) Freedom Summer Photographs. The University of Southern Mississippi Libraries, McCain Library and Archives.

Figure 6-1: The Full Circling photograph (*Mobile Street Looking South*) Herbert Randall (1964)

FULL CIRCLING: THE PROCESS

Full circling, as one form of visual literacy, is a multilayered process that, at its core, uses visual media as text to be read and interpreted. It is an active process because unlike watching film—which can be a solitary act—this is visual technology that is "socially applied knowledge and it is social conditions which make the crucial difference in how it is applied" (Kress 1998, 53, 54). Its purpose is to engage a classroom of students in what I call arts-based activism—that is, to question, reflect, actively listen, exchange dialogue, communicate, dramatize, and *transmediate* what they have learned—"take what [they] know in one sign system and recast it in another" (Suhor 1992, cited in Harste 2001, 1)—as burgeoning advocates of human rights.

By beginning and ending with the same visual (and returning to it numerous times throughout the process), the students come "full circle." What lies within the circle —i.e., that which is scaffolded alongside the photograph—is a pastiche of additional photographs, authentic documents, paintings, collages, and other images that can be read and interpreted along with traditional fiction and nonfiction narratives from a specific time in history. Then, woven within these historical layers are places for drama, where students can use their imaginations to become some of the characters they have met along the way and "see how it feels" (Heathcote [1976] 1989, 54).

Full circling comprises four steps:

Step One: Start with a visual and ask students to see and question mindfully—to be curious and wonder.
Step Two: Ask students to become aware of the text emotionally and respond in kind.
Step Three: Engage students by using dramatic activities and fictional characters to observe, evaluate, and act on narrative conflicts—to explore human rights as multiple perspectives.
Step Four: Return students full circle as they transmediate what was learned.

Each of these steps builds on the step before it—that is, students begin to read and interpret both cognitively and affectively (with the head and the heart), step-by-step, in a process that invites "expressive engagements [that] help students make deeply personal, introspective, and emotive connections between new information and themselves—and these engagements allow them to internalize information" (Bustle 2004, 421). The essence of full circling, however—that which occurs before the process is set in motion—is the teacher's selection of a historical event or time period and the gathering of materials that accompany it. This essential step of organizing and orchestrating—which visual media and which narratives are selected and how they will be used together—is critical to increasing the potential for greater student meaning-making once the process begins. The following is my full circling process.

FULL CIRCLING IN ACTION

My work with the students in Mrs. Jennings's (pseudonym) fifth-grade classroom occurred a short time after they read Christopher Paul Curtis' *The Watsons Go to Birmingham—1963*. Unlike other times when I used the full circling process, these twenty-one African American students had a context for what I was about to offer. They had read a piece of historical fiction that centered on a time in American history that we could explore from multiple perspectives. They had also done some research and had discussions on segregation in the early 1960s as extensions of Black History Month. For my part, I selected materials that I thought—when combined with their previous knowledge—would give the students new information with which to participate in a more profound way.

I specifically chose this particular historical time period—called Freedom Summer—for two reasons. First, I wanted a time in history in which we could examine the courage of African American people. After the 1964 Civil Rights Act was passed it was often not recognized by whites, especially in the South. And, second, as a white woman who has spent many years working in the performing arts as a foundation to social and political activism, I wanted to continue to scrutinize Ladson-Billings' (1995, 1998) ideas of culturally responsive teaching. By inviting the students to develop a "sociopolitical consciousness or an activist's civic and social awareness" (262) in examining and then becoming the people who lived Freedom Summer in 1964, I believed the students would also make historical memories that could positively impact their understanding of themselves today.

I arrived on a cold March morning with all the materials I had prepared for my work with the children. Having chosen Freedom Summer in Mississippi as my historical event, I brought with me approximately twenty black-and-white overheads, among them the Randall full circle photograph (see Figure 6–1), as well as examples of racist (Jim Crow) advertisements and signage (white-only restrooms, bath houses, etc.). In addition, I had color overheads of Jacob Lawrence's paintings—among them *Freedom to Vote*—and copies of authentic documents such as (1) a Student Non Violent Coordinating Committee (SNCC) brochure asking for funds to support its Mississippi Freedom Project: "*$5.00 will supply school materials for one day-student for one semester; $25 will pay the utility bills for one Freedom School for one semester*"; (2) an excerpt from a young white SNCC student volunteer who wrote to his parents about an incident with voter registration in Mississippi: "*We *got about 14 Negroes to go to the court house with the intention of registering to vote. Sheriff Smith greeted the party with a six shooter drawn from his pocket, and said 'Okay, who's first?' Most of the Negroes remained cautiously quiet. After several seconds a man who had never before been a leader stepped up to the Sheriff, smiled and said, 'I'm first, Hartman Turnbow'"*; and (3) excerpts from the SNCC Security Handbook: *"Do not stand in doorways at night with the light at your back. At night, people should not sit in their rooms without drawn shades. Do not congregate in front of the house at night. Make sure doors have locks and are locked. Carry identification at all times. Keep children safe at all cost."*

Also, I had several traditional narratives to read aloud, including Deborah Wiles' *Freedom Summer*, a fictional tale of John Henry (a black boy) and Joe (a white boy) who are friends in 1964 Mississippi; plus several pieces of nonfiction—testimony from African American men and women who recounted stories of racism in the South from their youth (Chafe, Gavins, and Korstad 2001; Hampton and Fayer 1990).

My plan was to give the students a balanced experience that would both heighten and extend their knowledge of African American courage during the civil rights movement, while offering them opportunities to react, reflect, assess, dialogue, imagine, and communicate what they were seeing, feeling, and questioning in a human rights venue as we worked through the full circling process.

Without a great deal of explanation (other than to tell the fifth-graders I would begin and end with a photograph from 1964 Mississippi, and I wanted them to ask questions, to make guesses, and to explore with me), I presented the full circle photograph and asked my first questions: "What do you see? Tell me everything you are noticing." And I made an initial list of their responses on chart paper.

STUDENT: There's a bench, some bushes and a tree.
TRISHA: A bench, some bushes and a tree. Okay. What else?
STUDENT: The buildings are really close together.
STUDENT: There are a lot of boxes on the ground.
TRISHA: Why do you think that is?
STUDENT: Are they taking out the trash?
TRISHA: Umhmmm . . . yes, maybe it's trash day.
STUDENT: And there are stairs there.
TRISHA: I wonder where the stairs go? (I say, but by now the photograph is conjuring up plenty of dialogue without me, and my question goes unanswered.)

94 FULL CIRCLING

STUDENT: Oh wait. I think I see a dog.
STUDENT: But what about the boy?
STUDENT: That's not a boy. That's a girl. She has on a skirt.
STUDENT: No. That's definitely a boy. He has a baseball cap on.
STUDENT: Oh . . . yeah. I see.
STUDENT: There's a car at the end of the street and I think I see someone staring at him.
STUDENT: Hey . . . there's a City Beauty Salon *and* a Beauty Shop.
STUDENT: Yeah, but one has a barber pole.
STUDENT: Na-uh.
STUDENT: Ya-huh. See right there? (and he points to it)
STUDENT: Oh . . . yeah. I see.

I began by honoring everything the students said to validate their responses, but after a while they no longer needed me. The text questioning continued and multiple dialogues began to take place. The students began to rely on one another to sort through what they were noticing, and I saw that socially applied knowledge, in the form of inquiry, was taking place. "Those who assume a questioning stance," say Berghoff and others (2000) "depend upon conversations with others . . ." (ix).

Step one of full circling—to see and question mindfully; to be curious and to wonder—had begun. The students had started to *access information* both internally (prior knowledge) and externally (taking a visual image and beginning to unpack its meaning, much as a good reader would unconsciously do with a traditional text). In defining visual media as a role in literacy education, Flood, Lapp, and Bayles-Martin (2000) refer to accessing information as one of "at least six process components [that] provide a useful framework for understanding the ways in which people develop communication skills" (67). By asking a simple open-ended question (What are you noticing?) I was able to encourage the children to "access their own personal knowledge and that of their peers" (68) so that, together, they could begin to read and interpret the Randall photograph as text and have an initial dialogue about it.

Step two of full circling—to become aware of the text emotionally and respond in kind—would now link the reading of the photograph as a text to the students' hearts. After the initial photograph discussion, the students were asked to use their imaginations as they listened to authentic testimony from women and men who were young during Freedom Summer. By conjuring a visual impression of the person talking, the children were asked to feel what they, themselves, might have felt during that time, if they had been present.

What follows is one of several excerpts (testimonies) that were read. Each excerpt was read twice: The first time so that the students could listen to it with their eyes closed and become aware of the text meaningfully; and the second time (as another means of affective awareness) to hear the text while I showed photographs, paintings, and signage—a Coca-Cola advertisement, a "colored" entrance to a department store, etc.—that either supported segregation or, like Lawrence's paintings or Beardon's collages, purposefully (and with great irony) brought its deleterious effects to our attention.

Testimony of Arial Barnes

While I was living in Hattiesburg—this would have been in my late teens, I guess, it was strictly segregated. Segregation was never really explained to me. I just came up sort of knowing what it was, you know. It was just there. We would meet White girls on the street and we just knew to move on over. I remember going to a movie with a girlfriend of mine and somehow my friend bumped up against a White girl. And when she did, the young man taking tickets said, "Watch it, there." And my girlfriend said, "Same here." Oh my goodness, the young White man was awfully peeved and when we were going in, she ran. Didn't realize, you know, what she had said, and she got scared that he would wallop her so she ran. We teased her about it, but it wasn't funny because he really meant business. He was going to strike her if she had stood there, you know. Incidents like that made me feel angry. You wondered why you couldn't be treated, you know, as a person. But people were just afraid to stand up for themselves. You didn't know who you could count on. (Hampton and Fayer 1990)

I placed the original full circle photograph back up and asked the students to move into pairs and reflect on what they had just seen and heard. I told them not to rush but to take their time and not speak their word(s) until they knew they were ready. "These words," I said, "should be *feeling words* that best describe the [Randall] photograph now that you have more information about the time and what black people were up against in 1964." I wrote their responses down on the same chart paper, right alongside their first comments. The words came slowly at first with one voice—"SAD"—then two—"DISAPPOINTED . . . HORRIBLE" . . . and gradually the pace quickened until multiple voices were speaking as one: "SEGREGATED, DEPRESSED, UNFAIR, ENRAGED, RACIST, UNJUST, SCARED, THREATENED, MISERABLE, DIRTY, UNWANTED, TERRIFIED, OUTRAGED."

It is clear that the students made many multilateral connections to the testimonies and visuals that were read in step two of the process. Here, all the combined passages—the original full circle photograph, the negative signage and advertisements, Lawrence's paintings, Beardon's collages, and the authentic testimonies—are simultaneously being read and reflected upon as text. Unlike the role of some illustrations to a text "where the written text fully carries all the information, and the image 'repeats' that information" (Kress 1998), each image offered in step two stands on its own, with the spoken narrative, inviting "both writing and image [to be equally] informative" (64).

Obviously the differences in the responses from step one to step two (as they are from each step to the next) are due, in part, to the fact that with each step the children's work deepened. In step one, the students used inquiry to notice and wonder about what was going on with the photograph. They positioned themselves outside the photograph and looked in (Edmiston and Long 1999). In step two, they saw authentic advertisements and other images of segregation as well as heard people talk about what it was like in Mississippi—about the ways in which racism damaged their lives and the lives of their families, friends, and community. And the students moved in a bit closer. Although they still stood outside the photograph looking in, they certainly felt more connected to the downtown street in Randall's photograph. They began to identify with the young man walking down the street, and their sense of justice versus injustice was heightened. The power with which they described the combined texts in step two—using words like *dirty, outraged, threatened,* and *unwanted*—clearly points to the fact that blending visual and written texts as arts-based activism can "serve as expressive scaffolding that taps emotive and affective ways of knowing so that students can begin to make empathetic connections to human rights' issues" (Bustle 2004, 421).

Step three of full circling—using dramatic activities and fictional characters to observe, evaluate, and act on narrative conflicts—now positioned the students in such a way that they could move *inside* the

Randall photograph. They became characters who experienced, through drama, conflicts similar to that which the boy in the photograph certainly faced. For this step, I chose to read aloud a fictional text, Deborah Wiles' *Freedom Summer* (2001). In this narrative, there are two major conflicts involving segregation. The first occurs when, thirsty after a swim in the creek, John Henry (an African American boy) cannot enter Mr. Mason's (a white man's) store to buy an ice pop with Joe (his white friend) because "he's not allowed." This is where I stopped reading the text, and the children and I had a conversation about what the conflict was:

STUDENT 1: John Henry can't go into that guy's store because he's black.
STUDENT 2: Well that's not fair.
TRISHA: No, it's not, but you know that although the Civil Rights Act was passed, there were many white people who didn't accept it, right? Remember how we talked about that before I started reading the story? So that means that in the South, folks who were not white, like me, were considered "less than . . ."
STUDENT 3: human . . .?
TRISHA: (hesitated) yeah . . .
STUDENT 1: So he can't go in that guy's . . .
STUDENT 2: Mr. Mason's . . .
STUDENT 1: Yeah, Mr. Mason's store, and Joe can go right in because he's white, and John Henry's gotta wait outside.
TRISHA: Yep. That's pretty much how it was.

At this point, I wanted to move from conversation—dialogues with me, and other children in pairs and trios talking—into personal reflection and exploration. I asked the students to close their eyes and *picture* the conflict, inside and outside Mr. Mason's store. I urged them to reflect further. "What might the conflict have looked like? What might it have sounded like? What might it have felt like? Who might have been present?" After a few moments, "when you have a clear picture in your mind," I asked them to open their eyes, and describe and share what they saw. As everyone shared their images of the conflict, I put up a writable transparency and we began to construct a fused character map (see Figure 6–2) with Mr. Mason in the middle (as the source of the conflict). Interestingly, many characters, in addition to the main characters, appeared—from the customers inside Mr. Mason's store, to the people outside riding on the bus, or driving by in their cars, to cats in the alley.

Figure 6-2: Character Map

With the character map completed, we were ready to move into the world of the imaginal, where the children could "generate a dramatic 'elsewhere,' a fictional world, which will be inhabited for the insights, interpretations, and understandings it may yield" (O'Neill 1995, 12).

I told the students that my colleague, whom I positioned in the front of the room, represented the conflict. Then I had them look at the character map we had just constructed, select a character whom they felt a positive or negative attachment to—one that they would like to *see how it feels* to become, and then position themselves as that character *in relationship to the conflict*. In this way, the children were able to make choices and experience the conflict from multiple perspectives and points of view, but in an environment where it was safe for them to do so.

Here, I used still image construction (also called tableau or frozen picture) to enable the children "to strengthen the reflective element of their work" (O'Neill 1995, 126). With this strategy, the children created a picture in time of what the conflict looked like to them using the characters from our character map. "The selective use of tableau," says O'Neill,

> as a unit of activity . . . releases participants from the demands of action, requires deliberate composition, embodies understanding, manifests meaning, allows time to be frozen or recalled, permits a level of abstraction to enter the work, and shapes and shares both information and insight. (127)

Before they moved into place, I asked some (rhetorical) questions guided by the work of Dorothy Heathcote ([1976] 1989). "What will your character's impression of this conflict be? From where you are standing or sitting, how will *you as your character* see the conflict? If you are with Mr. Mason in his store, will you view the conflict differently than if you are riding by in a bus or in a car or if you're an animal in the alley? Do you think this conflict might be resolved? These are the things you should reflect upon, and also the things we need to see in your bodies and in your faces—in you—when we do still image. Okay?"

Although none of the children had previous experiences with still image construction, they moved quickly into place. I was taken by the fact that there was no rush to become the three main characters, but rather, these fifth-graders' interest seemed to be piqued by the opportunity to portray the unspoken or implied characters during the moment of conflict. The image that they created was stunning. Without many words shared among them, seven children pulled and pushed desks into place and formed a bus. Three children got down on all fours and cowered in a corner as alley cats. Several children got into their cars and began to drive (at various points) along the street. There were several more children inside Mr. Mason's store—some closer to Joe and some closer to Mason. And others were outside in close proximity to John Henry, who waited patiently for his friend to return.

Once the still image, or tableau, was in place, I told the children to keep their positions but look quietly around the room so that they could see how their character map of the conflict had come to life. "This is a remarkable image," I said to them, "very, very powerful. But now I want to *hear* what happens when we bring your image, your *photograph* to life. So I'm going to come around and tap you on the shoulder and when I do, I want you to say what's on your mind about what you've just witnessed." As I walked solemnly around the room and tapped each child on the shoulder, some slowly and some quickly—a symphony of voices emerged.

From the bus driver: "I've been drivin' this bus for seven years and I seen this kind of thing happen all the time. It makes me mad."

From the passengers on the bus:

"What a rude owner."
"He's just a little boy."
"No he didn't just do that to that kid."
"I'll never spend my money there again."
"How could he?"
"When will this end?"

And from the people on the street:

(going in to Mason's): "Watch it, boy."
JOHN HENRY'S FATHER (in a proud voice): "That's my *son*."
ANNIE MAY (John Henry's mother): "Why did you do this to my baby?"

To the drivers who drove along the street:

"I drive my car past here every day and I always see this."
"Why can't that kid go to his own store?"

From the people in Mason's store:

"You black Negro look so plain, and lonely and ugly."
"I work for Mr. Mason. Keep these Negroes out of here."
"He done this for five weeks."
"You are mean and bad."
JOE: "I wish it was different."
MR. MASON: "I'm havin' a talk with this boy's daddy."

To the alley cats:

"Mr. Mason's mean when I come past. He give me the boot."
"He make me sick."
"That's not right."

Giving voice to the still image (as the final part of step three) propelled our work forward. Here, the students moved from reflection (where they created a mental picture of the conflict) through assessment (where the children graphed the images they had reflected upon to make the characters more concrete), to observation (where they chose who to become and gave those choices life), and, finally, to the first stages of activism (where their characters each expressed their point of view in relation to the narrative conflict). The significance of using drama in step three as a means to explore human rights is that "not only can students engage in *talk* about action—moral reasoning about what they *might* do if they were people in particular circumstances—in drama students take action and in imagination *do* that which in discussion they might only sketchily contemplate" (Wilhelm and Edmiston 1998, 59).

Step four of full circling—to return full circle and transmediate what was learned—offers the students a culminating event in which they can gather everything they have learned in steps one through three and recast it in another sign system. With these urban students, I chose to do this by creating *bio poetry*, in which the students, as the characters they portrayed in the still image, began by writing down their feelings about the event that just took place, and eventually, in small groups, created a poem together.

I wanted the students to eventually write their poems in small supportive groups to help one another find and cultivate their ensemble voices, as well as raise the (imagined) voices of the African American people who lived Freedom Summer forty years before.

However, as we drew near to step four (the final step in the full circling process), the bell rang, signaling that my time with the students had ended. "Oh . . ." I said, "I actually had one more thing to do, but I guess we don't have time for it." Mrs. Jennings said that the students "had gym class next, but . . ." "*We'll* stay!" the children said. And so they did, and I placed the full circle photograph on the overhead one last time as the children were invited to write reflective poems about their experiences. The missed gym class turned into a wellspring of resonant student poetry, rife with the history and the lives of the people who inhabited the images of Freedom Summer.

And folded into the crevices of the full circle photograph's boxes (which might be trash going out) and the buildings (which were close together), and the two beauty parlors (one with a barber pole), and the stairs that had no ending, and the cars parked here and there, were also the young lives of twenty-one urban fifth graders who had seen and felt and made history with the young boy walking down the street in rural Hattiesburg, Mississippi, in 1964.

EPILOGUE

In this chapter, I have detailed my work with a process that I implemented in an urban fifth-grade classroom called *full circling*. Although full circling is my design, its inherent principles and strategies have been influenced by other scholars' work in the fields of drama education (Booth and Neelands 1998; Fines and Verrier 1974; Edmiston 1998; Edmiston and Long, 1999; Heathcote [1976] 1989, 1995; Manley and O'Neill 1997; O'Neill 1995; Taylor 1996, 1998; Wilhelm and Edmiston 1998); literacy and the use of multiple ways of making meaning (Harste, Short, and Burke 1996; Berghoff, Egawa, Harste, and Hoonan 2000); and culturally responsive teaching (Banks and McGee Banks 1997; Delpit 1988, 1995; Freire 1974; hooks 1993; Ladson-Billings 1995, 1998).

The idea for full circling came about a few years ago while I was participating in a joint research project using drama with urban fourth-graders (Wies Long & Gove, 2003/04). It was then that I noticed that the children (a great many of whom were struggling readers and writers) *always* responded both eloquently and passionately when given a visual to jump-start our work together. This, combined with my ongoing observations of students with their teacher—and the realization that they did much better with comprehension whenever there were pictures that also informed the text(s) they were reading—led me to think about how I might better combine authentic visuals with the methodologies I was already using (multiple literacies with drama at its center) to enhance the students' potential for greater meaning-making overall. Would historically contextualized, authentic visuals further motivate students to read, write, speak, listen, reflect, and act as critical respondents? Would the addition of authentic visuals (photographs, paintings, documents, etc.) that were "read" with historically situated fiction and nonfiction in a multiple literacy setting (that is, an environment where students were encouraged to question, read, write, reflect upon, and dramatize the world of the text) stimulate students sufficiently to (1) engage them in a critical period of American history and (2) add to their overall scholarship? Would they be better writers because they not only understood the lives of African Americans in history, but also *became* them? And would they develop what Ladson-Billings (1998) refers to as "a sociopolitical consciousness"—an "activist's civic and social awareness" (262)?

Having worked with the fifth-graders for only a short while, it is difficult to say how the work impacted their academic lives overall.

However, as revealed in one child's poetry, I can say with great certainty that using multiple literacies with authentic visuals "read" as text developed in the students a sense of responsibility for who they were as African American people in history:

> BLACKS WHERE [WERE] NOT BEING TREATING [TREATED] THE SAME AS WHITES. SEGREGATION MUST END IN PEACE.
>
> We are all human beans (beings)
> so why can't we use the same things
> We fought for our rights every day and night
> Blacks should be treated the same
> No fussing, bad language, or fights
> We all are like each other so
> Why can't we get alone (along) with one another?

REFERENCES

Banks, James A., and CherryMcGee Banks. 1997. *Multicultural education: Issues and Perspectives*. Boston: Allyn & Bacon.

Beardon, Romare 1964. "Watchin' the Good Trains Go By." Photomontage and mixed media on paper.

Berghoff, Barbarba., Kathryn A. Egawa, Jerome C. Harste, and Barry T. Hoonan. 2000. *Beyond Reading and Writing: Inquiry, Curriculum and Multiple Ways of Knowing*. Urbana, IL: NCTE.

Booth, David., and Jonothan Neelands, eds. 1998. *Writing in Role: Classroom Projects Connecting Writing and Drama*. Hamilton, ON: Caliburn Enterprises Inc.

Bustle, Lynn S. 2004. "The Role of Visual Representation in the Assessment of Learning." *Journal of Adult & Adolescent Literacy* 47: 418–423.

Chafe, William H., Raymond Gavins, and Robert Korstad, eds. 2001. *Remembering Jim Crow: African Americans Tell About Life in the Segregated South*. New York: The New Press.

Christensen, Linda. 2000. *Reading, Writing, and Rising Up: Teaching About Social Justice and the Power of the Written Word*. Milwaukee, WI: Rethinking Schools Publications.

Curtis, Christopher Paul. 1998. *The Watsons Go to Birmingham, 1963*. New York: Holt, Rinehart & Winston.

Delpit, Lisa. (1988). "The Silenced Dialogue: Power and Pedagogy in Educating Other People's Children." *Harvard Educational Review* 59 (3): 280–298.

———. (1995). *Other People's Children*. New York: The Free Press.

Edmiston, Brian. 1998. "The A, B, C of Drama." *Drama Matters: The Journal of the Ohio Drama Exchange* 3: 49–59.

Edmiston, Brian, and Trisha Wies Long. 1999. *Reading Texts Inside Out: Engagement and Interpretation with Drama*. Unpublished manuscript for Teaching and Learning with Drama courses. Columbus, OH: The Ohio State University.

Fines, J., and R. Verrier. 1974. *The Drama of History: An Experiment in Co-operative Teaching*. London: New University Education Press.

Flood, James, Diane Lapp, and Debra Bayles-Martin. 2000. "The Role of Visual Media in Literacy Education." In *What Counts as Literacy: Challenging the School Standard*, edited by M. A. Gallego and S. Hollingworth, 62–84. New York: Teachers College Press.

Freire, Paulo. 1974. *Pedagogy of the Oppressed*. New York: Seabury.

Hampton, Henry and Steve Fayer. 1990. *Voices of Freedom: An Oral History of the Civil Rights Movement from the 1950s Through the 1980s*. New York: Bantam.

Harste, Jerome C., Kathy G. Short, and Carolyn Burke. 1996. *Creating Classrooms for Authors: The Reading-Writing Connection*. Portsmouth, NH: Heinemann.

Heard, Georgia 1999. *Awakening the Heart: Exploring Poetry in Elementary and Middle School*. Portsmouth, NH: Heinemann.

Heathcote, Dorothy. [1976] 1989. "Drama as a Process for Change." In *Dorothy Heathcote: Collected Writings on Education and Drama*, edited by Liz Johnson and Cecily O'Neill, 26–40. London, England: Hutchinson.

Heathcote, Dorothy, and Gavin Bolton. 1995. *Drama for Learning: Dorothy Heathcote's Mantle of the Expert Approach to Education*. Portsmouth, NH: Heinemann.

hooks, bell. 1993. "Transformative Pedagogy and Multiculturalism." In *Freedom's Plow: Teaching in Multicultural Classrooms*, edited by Theresa Perry and James W. Fraser. New York: Routledge.

Kress, Gunther. 1998. "Visual and Verbal Modes of Representation in Electronically Mediated Communication: The Potential of New Forms of Text." In *Page to Screen* by I. Snyder, 53–79. London: Routledge.

Ladson-Billings, Gloria (1995). "Toward a Theory of Culturally Relevant Pedagogy." *American Educational Research Journal* 32(3) 465–491.

REFERENCES

———. 1998. "Teaching in Dangerous Times: Culturally Relevant Approaches to Teacher Assessment." *The Journal of Negro Education* 67 (3): 255–267.

Lawrence, Jacob. From The Migration Series: *The Ironers*, 1943 (Private Collection); *Migration of the Negro*, 1940–41; and *Freedom to Vote*, 1959. The Phillips Collection, Washington, D.C.

Long, Trisha Wies. 2001. *How to Use Engagement Strategies in the Urban Classroom*. Unpublished manuscript for Literature-based Reading Methods for Children [and Young Adults]. Cleveland, OH: Cleveland State University.

Long, Trisha Wies and Mary Kay Gove. 2003/04. "How Engagement Strategies and Literature Circles Promote Critical Response in a Fourth-Grade Urban Classroom." *The Reading Teacher* 57: 350–361.

Manley, A., and Cecily O'Neill, eds. 1997. *Dreamseekers: Creative Approaches to the African American Heritage*. Portsmouth, NH: Heinemann.

Murray, Donald. 1985. "What Happens when Students Learn to Write." In *Breaking Ground: Teachers Relate Reading and Writing in the Elementary School*, edited by Jane Hansen, Thomas Newkirk, and Donald Graves, 201. Portsmouth, NH: Heinemann.

O'Neill, Cecily. 1995. *Drama Worlds: A Framework for Process Drama*. Portsmouth, NH: Heinemann.

Piro, J. M. 2000. "The Picture of Reading: Deriving Meaning in Literacy Through Image." *The Reading Teacher* 56: 126–134.

Taylor, Phillip ed. 1996. *Researching Drama and Arts Education*. London: Falmer Press.

———. 1998. *Redcoats and Patriots: Reflective Practice in Drama and Social Studies*. Portsmouth, NH: Heinemann.

Wiles, Deborah. 2001. *Freedom Summer*. New York: Atheneum Books for Young Readers.

Wilhelm, Jeffrey D., and Brian Edmiston. 1998. *Imagining to Learn: Inquiry, Ethics, and Integration Through Drama*. Portsmouth, NH: Heinemann.

7

"Always Listen to Children": Process Drama as a Site for Fostering Freedom, Voice, and Choice

Jenifer Jasinski Schneider

Giving students the freedom to make suggestions in the classroom contributes to their writing. When you accept their suggestions it makes them feel valuable and important—which also helps writing. It helps create that whole atmosphere of risk taking. So peace and respect in all areas helps writing. (Interview with Sondra, September 6.)

I entered Sondra Stevens's (pseudonyms used for all names) classroom in order to conduct a descriptive and interpretive study of her writing instruction and the writing strategies of her second- and third-grade students. After several days of observation I realized that writing occurred throughout the day across many contexts—including process drama.

I also noticed that one characteristic of Sondra's teaching greatly impacted her writing instruction and was central to her work with drama: Sondra possessed an interactional style that empowered the students and allowed them to express their opinions. In other words, Sondra gave the students freedom, voice, and choice. She believed in a student-centered classroom in which the children were active, powerful, and critical members whose opinions and thoughts were respected and valued, not just during writing time, but throughout the day. Sondra was a "transformative intellectual" who was able to "treat students as critical agents, question how knowledge is produced and distributed, utilize dialogue, and make knowledge meaningful, critical, and ultimately emancipatory" (Giroux and McLaren 1986, 215). Sondra exhibited her abilities as a transformative intellectual most often through her use of process drama.

In this chapter, I reveal those tenets of Sondra's instruction that allowed her to create an empowering classroom environment. First, I describe Sondra's use of process drama as a classroom context for learning. Second, I identify the ways in which Sondra supported freedom, voice, and choice. Third, I juxtapose her ability to create an empowering classroom environment with her position as classroom "authority," and I critically examine the effects of freedom, voice, and choice on the individuals who were in this classroom.

PROCESS DRAMA AS A CONTEXT FOR LEARNING

Throughout the school year, Sondra engaged twenty-five second- and third-grade students in two process drama units, each lasting approximately three months.

The Peace Mission

In the first drama, Sondra asked the students to join her on a mission to spread peace throughout the world, and she solicited their involvement through a newspaper ad. The students replied to the ad by attending an orientation meeting (i.e., morning circle time) during which they were informed of the mission and its requirements—travel across the earth to find a peaceful new land. *If* the students successfully completed this dangerous journey, they would establish a new civilization for the purpose of spreading peace throughout the world. At the first meeting, the children were placed into groups so they could identify their individual strengths and then work toward the peace mission goals as a team. They also kept "Peace Diaries" so they could write about their thoughts and feelings over the course of the mission.

After a few days of building the students' background and belief in the drama, Sondra asked the students to invent obstacles, which would be combined to create a map for their journey. In addition to drawing the obstacles, Sondra asked the students to write a paragraph describing their own obstacles.

SONDRA: Right now, outside the drama, I want you to create the obstacles on the journey. I want you to draw the map that's going to be used. Each person will draw one picture of an obstacle that we will put on the map. For example, if you say that there is quicksand, you will draw the whole area of quicksand, write underneath "quicksand," and then turn it in. All those obstacles will be put together in a map form. I'll shape it like a map and then we will choose which route to go on. We may have to go on several different ones. OK, so just to make sure everyone understands, tell me one obstacle that we could have on our map.
CHILD: A snake pit.
SONDRA: OK, a huge pit with thousands of poisonous snakes. Now remember, maps have not only flatlands, they have mountains. You could think about all things in geography. What are things on maps all of the time?
CHILD: Roads.
SONDRA: Well nobody has been there enough to build roads. I'm talking about nature things.

> The children gave the following responses: lakes, grass, trees, oceans, mountains, volcanoes, rock slides, vines, forests, mud. Sondra wrote these on the chart. (Observation, September 13.)

Sondra assembled the individual obstacles into a large map of the landscape. The students took the map to dance class where Rachel, the dance teacher, used the peace journey as an opportunity to teach the students various types of body movements and the written representation of those movements, which are called motifs. Rachel explained the written symbols and then the students created their own actions for the symbols. Rachel's ideas helped Sondra realize that the students could actually depict their journey through motifs and the children could perform their journey through symbolic body movements.

After many weeks of preparation, the day of the journey finally arrived. The students choreographed and performed a dance that simulated their journey to the new land, called "Peace Valley." After becoming accustomed to life in this new land, the children decided to create the Peaceful Toy Company (PTC). Through this company, the children designed, manufactured, and distributed toys that were intended to spread peace throughout the world. As a culminating activity, they created the Peace Valley Newspaper, in which they wrote articles about their mission and advertised the toys to the rest of the school.

The Immigrant Drama

In the second drama, Sondra asked the students to investigate immigration for the government. In the following excerpt, Sondra placed the students in the roles of reporters and asked them to perform various types of research for this immigrant investigation.

> Remember, we are pretending now, so you're in role. Close your eyes for a minute. When you open them I want you to be a grown-up reporter who is about to get an assignment that you have to fulfill for your job. Close your eyes, please. Open your eyes. Reporters, I will be Mrs. Stevens. (Reading) *Locate an immigrant from one of the following countries and interview that person. Obtain artifacts*—and I'm going to explain what an artifact is—*such as visas, clothing, diary pages, objects brought from the homeland. Please photograph the immigrants. This information will supply our government with necessary research for helping and understanding future immigrants. It will assist in determining changes in current immigration laws.* Now, what are they asking you to do? Raise your hand and you can be yourselves again to tell me what to do. What is your assignment?
>
> (Observation, November 27.)

As the drama progressed, the students read literature, shared their own family stories of immigration, and conducted various activities related to many immigrants' journeys. For example, the students completed interview questionnaires, created biographies of the immigrants, and wrote diary entries. The students visually transformed their classroom by creating a replica of the Statue of Liberty and converted their reading loft to an immigrant ship. After the students completed their reporter assignments, Sondra asked each child to switch roles and become the immigrant they were studying. The reporters entered a time machine and then assumed their new roles. As immigrants, the children completed activities to help them understand their new personae. They created family histories, applied for passports, completed a photo essay of their experiences using tableaux, and wrote letters to their homeland.

Throughout both dramas, Sondra read literature, provided demonstrations, and discussed possible drama events. She modeled how the students should write in various genres depending on their roles in the dramas. And she sustained the dramas by remaining in role herself, helping students perform and reflect upon their drama work, and following students' agendas within the drama frames.

FREEDOM, VOICE, AND CHOICE

In this section, I share three events that occurred across the peace and immigrant dramas to highlight the ways in which students were given freedom, voice, and choice in the classroom.

Scene 1: Focus on Freedom

When Sondra began the school year with the peace drama, she placed students in the "mantle of the expert" (Heathcote and Bolton 1995) by asking them to take on the roles of missionaries for peace. Once the children understood that they could take on the role of any adult, the children immediately played along.

KARLA: I'm very young, and I have a child. Do people usually die on this trip, or is it safe? (The class audibly gasped.)

SONDRA: Generally we have had very few casualties. We did have someone get caught in quicksand because he didn't follow directions. Then we had the one case where the lady slid down the mountain, but we don't know if she died, because we didn't follow her. How many of you are willing to take the challenge? (All children agreed.)

CEDRIC: I'm a baby.

SONDRA: Oh, babies can't come. OK, I'm out of drama role and I'm Sondra: all of you need to take the role of an adult or a teenager. OK, I'm back in my role. Now today we need to get organized for traveling . . .

After several more minutes of discussion, Karla decided to reconfigure her role.

KARLA: When I said I had a child, I meant I am pregnant.

SONDRA: Oh. Now that's . . . (children giggling). I have no problem with a pregnant woman. But the people in your group will have to agree that you can come, and I'm sure they will. (Karla's group members agreed.)

(Observation, September 11.)

In this situation, Sondra faced a choice in deciding which role could be altered even though both students attempted to push boundaries. Interestingly, Sondra supported Karla's role, which I interpreted as objectionable and problematic, and redirected Cedric's role, which I viewed as harmless.

For me, Karla's role was surprising. However, Sondra accepted the role and treated Karla seriously. Karla's decision to be "pregnant" pushed traditional classroom norms, but Sondra's reaction reinforced the freedom and acceptance the children received. There was no real reason why Karla could not pretend to be pregnant; after all, she was pretending to be an adult. Nonetheless, I felt the role was awkward. What would the other children think? What would the parents say? Wouldn't this role bring up the topic of sex? As I pondered these questions, I realized that the only real problem with this role existed within my adult conception of the circumstance. For Sondra, few subjects were taboo. She did not exercise her power as adult and teacher in order to censor Karla's ideas. She allowed Karla to retain her power to imagine and to take on a role because Karla was not really pregnant; she was only imagining. In contrast, Cedric's role would have restricted his participation in the learning and writing activities. As a baby, he would not be able to execute the peace mission, he would not be able to reflect on the process, and he would not be able to fully participate in the academic engagement of the drama. Therefore, Sondra made the decision that Cedric should select another role.

Following the introduction to the role-play, Sondra asked the children to reflect on their feelings and expectations for the trip by writing in their "Peace Diaries." In her own diary (see Figure 7–1), Karla extended her freedom from the drama into her writing. She created a "sort of" husband, further expanding her role and her writing possibilities.

Scene 2: Focus on Voice

Sondra's support of students' risk-taking in role set the precedent for students to freely express themselves and take risks in other situations. For example, in order to heighten the students' understanding of the immigrants' struggle, Sondra asked the children to create a photo essay on immigration using tableau (O'Neill 1995). Sondra intended for the photo essay to capture important immigrant events as well as provide the students with an opportunity to write in role. Sondra first shared an actual photo essay with the children in order for them to develop a sense about the genre. Then she began to discuss ideas they could incorporate into their tableaux. Their ideas would ultimately appear in the resulting photographs as well as in their accompanying essays.

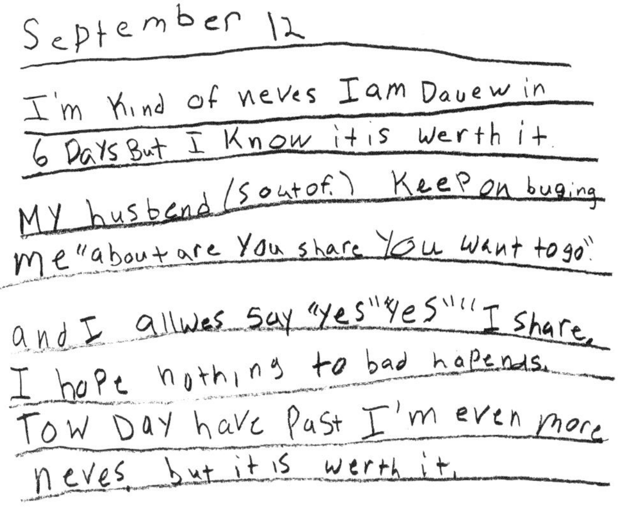

FREEDOM, VOICE, AND CHOICE 113

> September 12
>
> I'm kind of neves I am Davew in 6 Days But I Know it is werth it. MY husband (s out of.) Keep on buging me "about are You share You want to go" and I allwes say "yes" "yes" "I share. I hope nothing to bad hapends. Tow Day have Past I'm even more neves, but it is werth it.

Figure 7-1: Karla's Peace Diary

SONDRA: What is one thing that could be in a photo essay on immigration? What's one topic we should cover. We'll put them in order later, but what's one good idea? (Sondra wrote all ideas on chart paper.)

VINNIE: What it looks like on a street.

SONDRA: OK, I think that you're thinking that once they get there, the immigrants were in the streets. OK, I'll put that down.

KARLA: When they got to America, there were inspections, and someone like getting dragged away.

SONDRA: OK, like getting detained. Is that critical? So we want an Ellis Island scene that has to do with when you get there, how you get registered. What else? Now remember, all immigrants didn't come through Ellis Island, but that's important.

CHERYL: When I got there, I saw people walking to their new house.

SONDRA: You want people walking to their new house. Is that as critical as other things that happened to immigrants? We need six important aspects of immigrant life. We talked about once they get inside, but what about other things that are more critical?

CARTER: Like someone counting their coins.

SONDRA: OK, and that might happen at Ellis Island at the inspection. We'll let the Ellis Island group decide all the things that should go on in their picture, if someone wants to be counting coins, that's fine. I need to know what other scenes we want. We don't want two Ellis Island scenes, only one.

The photo essay discussion continued at great length. The students attempted to please Sondra by suggesting "critical" scenes, but all of their ideas related to Ellis Island. Clearly the students were affected by the information they learned about Ellis Island and the immigrants' struggles there. After a great deal of coaxing from Sondra, she finally recognized that the children were fascinated with Ellis Island, and she altered her ideas for the photo essay to accommodate their interests. Sondra told the class,

> OK, what I think I'm going to do, is allow each group to do the scene of your choice because you will each portray it differently. It will not tell a lot of different stories, but it might tell a lot of different people's stories. Maybe you remember how it was when people left and they got on the boat. You remember the deportation. So do what you want with your group, and we will write our essays to suit your needs as the authors of the picture. So the picture is going to control the words on this essay, and I'm not going to control your idea. We'll make it work by the title we choose. We will make it work by the way we put our stories together later. So everybody gets their way.
> (Observation, December 1.)

Although Sondra planned to focus on many immigration ideas, including leaving the homeland, arriving at Ellis Island, finding a job, and so on, the students expressed their opinions and negotiated ownership of the essay and, subsequently, the right to focus on Ellis Island.

Scene 3: Focus on Choice

During the immigrant drama, facts about the immigrants' struggles raised many issues and discussions about injustice, inequality, and prejudice. Sondra dealt with these issues in an open and reflective manner. She read stories about the immigrants—seeking children's literature that shared diverse perspectives on the events. In fact, one book stated that women were not allowed to attend the unveiling of the Statue of Liberty. When the students heard this, they were very surprised. An emotional discussion ensued when a group of boys laughed at the girls, stating that girls were not important enough to attend the celebration. Sondra told the class that women were not allowed to attend because men thought they would get trampled. Then Sondra asked the students to consider why the men would not get trampled as well. None of the students replied to this query, but a verbal argument ensued between the boys and the girls. At this point, Sondra asked the children to think about the issues.

SONDRA: We understand the emotion of the girls who say, "Wow, that wasn't fair," but I think the people who are male in our classroom should also be saying, "Wow, that wasn't fair." Because until we get boys to think about equal rights, then we're not getting anywhere. . . . [Whenever you] talk about the rights of any people, be they black people, white people, be they the rights of Jewish people, the rights of women, I hope that you support what is right and not just whatever you are. Because [if not] then all we do is create division. So when you hear that women could not attend the Statue of Liberty ceremony, then I think that the men should be as appalled as the women are.
VINNIE: But the women would have gotten trampled.
SONDRA: Vinnie, why would they get trampled and the men wouldn't?
VINNIE: Because men don't wear high heels that don't fit. (Vinnie stood up and wobbled around the circle of students.)
SONDRA: Women wore appropriate footwear for where they were. . . . But I'm not appreciating what I'm seeing. If you're really concerned about the historical facts about this, then you'll get serious. So I think that you have to give women enough respect that they wouldn't wear heels to the celebration if it was inappropriate to do so. So I don't think that's an appropriate response, Vinnie. You need to think about women as people with common sense.
ANGELA: Earl and Cedric [said], "I'm taking the women's side, and if they don't go, I'm not going."
SONDRA: Well, that was probably what some men felt at that time. Not all men were the ones who said the women couldn't come. It was some officials who said that. Now, just like not all whites wanted slavery—there were a lot of whites who said, "This is wrong"—there were a lot of men who said, "This is wrong." So we don't judge a whole group by what a majority is saying.
HEATHER: They should have thought how the women must have felt.
SONDRA: Right, and it was not thought about. And that's why today we're still dealing with women's rights, because it's been very slow changing.

(Observation, November 29.)

The previous excerpt reveals that Sondra was very conscious of her role in developing sensitive, thoughtful individuals who cared about others. Sondra made an important statement when she told her students that they should "support what is right and not just whatever [they] are." As Giroux (1987) states, Sondra engaged the students in a "project of possibility" in which she taught her students "not only to make choices and to think critically but to believe that they can make a difference in the world" (179).

Sondra's subsequent debate with Vinnie revealed that she thought he was wrong about women, and she publicly refuted his stance. Yet, although Sondra held the dominant "teacher role," throughout this exchange I believe Sondra engaged Vinnie and the other children in a dialogue, one in which she opened the possibilities for a more critical discussion of the inequities of the past—one in which she offered choices and alternatives for their decisions and behaviors. Even though Vinnie provided possible reasons for the exclusion of women from the celebration, he presented his argument in a facetious manner. He stood up and wobbled around as if wearing high heels. Given Vinnie's mocking portrayal of women, Sondra did not allow his choices to go unchallenged. When supporting equal rights, Sondra used her position of authority and asked Vinnie to reexamine his statements with facts in mind. Then Sondra led the conversation away from Vinnie and into a discussion of other injustices of the past. Sondra's goal was to promote basic human rights, and by acting as the teacher, she used Vinnie's statements as an opportunity for learning.

THE BALANCING ACT

In this section, I reveal how the students became aware of the power of their voices through interactions with, and acceptance from, adults and peers as they negotiated with each other. I reveal how the students were engaged in dialogic inquiry (Foucault 1972; Freire 1970) in which their voices were heard, examined, and also challenged as Sondra simultaneously empowered students and fostered their freedom, voices, and choices while ensuring a safe learning environment.

Relational Authority

Whether students in role were embarking on dangerous journeys or traveling across the Atlantic on immigrant ships, Sondra balanced the children's need for freedom and exploration with her need to assess their abilities and to facilitate and challenge their growth as learners. In this respect, Sondra functioned like Lensmire's (1997) "Dostoevskian novelist" in that she was a teacher "who creates a classroom-novel and takes up relations with student-characters" (368). She carefully crafted the learning contexts, her instruction for writing, and her relationship with individual students. Sondra explained this balance in the following interview.

> I think that at this level, the more freedom of choice they have, the more writing you're going to get and the more opportunity they have to practice. . . . you can easily shut down creativity with too many requirements. On the other hand, I think that we shouldn't underestimate their possibilities. So you still introduce them to all those particulars [skills]. . . . I'm trying to say that you should make the information available and push them as far as they can go, but at the same time leave them lots of freedom and room to create. . . . You're really working more for the expression of thought. That's the ultimate goal.
> (Interview, November 14.)

Sondra gave the students freedom, voice, and choice in the classroom, but she was also particular about the format of certain genres, the learning that was going to occur within drama work, and how certain activities were to be done in the classroom. I have identified and termed this aspect of Sondra's writing instruction as her "authority." Sondra shared the decision-making responsibility with the students. However, her acceptance of the students' decisions did not indicate that control and power issues were nonexistent. Sondra was most definitely exercising her position as teacher and authority. In the end, Sondra made decisions that supported students' learning, maintained the drama action, and fostered dramatic creativity over interference.

Although Sondra never lost sight of her responsibilities as a teacher, she was able to create roles for herself. Sondra made the dramas more believable because she was involved with the children *in role*, not as their teacher. And while Sondra frequently went in and out of role for many purposes, the children maintained a belief in her role and in the drama.

The children portrayed characters and wrote as characters different from themselves. At times they were children, at other times they were adults. They were peacemakers and immigrants. They were Sondra's students, but they were also her peers. And this unique relationship created boundary disputes in the classroom.

The Shifting of Power

In this classroom, freedom, voice, and choice created authority shifts. The students' empowered stances caused problems for Sondra. To illustrate this point, I recount two particular incidents that occurred.

During a whole class discussion, Sondra was called by the office and asked to send lunchroom helpers to the cafeteria to help the lunchroom director, Stephanie.

SONDRA: I'm not going to call people who are standing up. Now this is hard enough to choose. Stephanie doesn't want any problems . . . I'm going to send Janeen [Caucasian, female, second grade], and Heather [Caucasian, female, second grade], and I'm sending Patrick [Caucasian, male, third grade], and I'm sending Jia [African American, female, third grade], and I'm sending Kianna [African American, female, second grade].

KARLA: Is that all?

SONDRA: Yes.

EARL and MITCHELL: Man! Sondra!

SONDRA: That's OK. She'll ask us again sometime if we do a good job. (Several children continue to complain.) So I'm not going to talk about this anymore.

KARLA: Why did you pick them?

SONDRA: The kids down there—Stephanie doesn't have to say one time to be quiet while she's trying to talk, which I have to say to some of you. And it doesn't mean if you weren't picked, that you're one of those people. It's just that I couldn't pick everybody. And I think you know that, Karla. (inaudible discussion)

VINNIE: You picked all second-graders. Why didn't you pick third-graders?

SONDRA: Well, I didn't. I don't go by grade level, Vinnie. I go by who . . . (inaudible arguing) I have a rationale in my brain that goes through my brain when I pick people. When I looked at Kianna, I thought, "I never pick Kianna." Jia, because Jia will go down there and she will make everybody else work right. And who else did I pick?

EARL: That fat girl.

SONDRA: Oh, just a minute. Get out of here. (She pointed toward the coat closet/time-out room.) I'll talk to you later. I don't like that.
EARL: I didn't say anything.
SONDRA: Look at this. Come here a minute. (Reading from the civil rights chart). I have a right to be myself in this room. That means that no one will treat me unfairly because I'm black or white, fat or thin, short or tall, boy or girl. Never let me hear you call someone fat again. Ever. Because now you know we don't do that in here. (Sondra returned to a discussion about a book.)
(Observation, September 15.)

I was shocked by the reactions of the class and upset with the students for not showing Sondra the respect she deserved. I knew, based on our conversations, that Sondra was painfully aware of equality issues in classrooms, in schools, and in life. In this class, in particular, there was a mix of students from different socioeconomic classes, races, and ethnicities, and Sondra was a conscientious teacher who made explicit statements about fairness and equality. In fact, she frequently referred students to the civil rights that were posted on the wall. I never expected the children to direct accusations of bias toward Sondra. The children were wrong, and I wanted to tell them so. However, Sondra took an alternative route. She repeated her reasoning for choosing certain students, and then reassured the students that they would have their turn. The only time Sondra revealed anger was the moment Earl called another child "fat". Even then, she quickly abated her anger and redirected her approach with Earl. Sondra was upset, but instead of punishing Earl, she led him to question his statements.

Many weeks later, Sondra was in a similar situation. She asked for volunteers to work with the art teacher to create a Statue of Liberty replica for the immigrant drama. As the members were selected, some of the children accused Sondra of selecting only white children (Sondra is African American). Once again, Sondra explained her reasoning to the children. After continued complaints and allegations, Sondra became visibly upset. She told the children that she felt she was being harassed. She reminded the students that they were violating her civil rights, and eventually their criticism ceased.

Later that day, Sondra asked me, a Caucasian, if I noticed bias in her selection of children. I told her that I did not notice any bias and, in fact, I was upset by the incident. Sondra confided that the children's accusations were very upsetting to her as well. She stated that she had a difficult time continuing the conversation with them because she was almost to the point of crying.

When I saw how hurt Sondra was, my initial reaction was that there was a limit to how much voice she should allow children to have in the classroom. These children were not able to reason like adults, and therefore, they should not always be in charge; they could not handle the freedom. Maybe process drama should be restricted to use with very clear-cut, teacher-controlled topics that allowed for imagining without the resistance. However, with continued observations, I eventually changed my mind. Giving students a *true* voice, and opportunities to make choices to use that voice, was the power of Sondra's teaching. She believed so strongly in allowing the students to express themselves and make choices that she was willing to accept their criticism and challenges. Upon reflection, I now believe that the students' accusations were another manifestation of their freedom, voice, and choice. Sondra wanted the students to express themselves even if she became the victim of the power differential she created.

CONCLUSIONS AND IMPLICATIONS

Although I entered this classroom to study writing, I learned much about writing outside of those intended contexts. This teacher's support of writers required more than allowing students to take risks during "writing" time. It required that the students and the teacher take risks all day. Freedom, voice, and choice were not relegated or confined to certain times or situations. Children's risk taking was not an isolated writing skill. Rather, children felt empowered and knew that their voices were valuable throughout the day, across all situations. As Freire (1970) stated, "The teacher cannot think for her students, nor can she impose her thought on them. Authentic thinking, thinking that is concerned about *reality*, does not take place in ivory tower isolation, but only in communication" (58).

Teachers, administrators, school boards, and curriculum guides impose substantial agendas on elementary schools and classroom pedagogy, yet there is room for flexibility and change. If teachers can accommodate a last-minute assembly on fire safety, then they can accommodate a student's new idea for a change in classroom activities. However, providing students with freedom, voice, and choice in the classroom is not devoid of some chaos, disrespect, and time off-task.

CONCLUSIONS AND IMPLICATIONS **121**

Figure 7-2: Molly's advice to future teachers

Sondra's classroom was not perfect; however, Sondra interacted with students in ways that I had never witnessed nor practiced myself. I saw students willing to express their ideas even when they knew they were "objectionable." I saw students think, hold conversations, and actually have a voice, not only in their daily experiences, but in their own learning processes.

A student may enter a classroom with a voice, but the situations in which that voice may be heard are usually developed and arranged by a teacher. Therefore, it is vitally important that teachers recognize the need for students to have opportunities to develop and share their individual voices throughout the events of the school day. Process drama provides a site of possibility for the type of self-expression, imagination, and creativity that children need while also providing a context for integrated teaching and learning.

Freedom, voice, and choice were fostered through Sondra's consistent respect for children, her varied strategies, contexts, and guidelines, and her ability to use process drama as a tool for learning. There is no truer testament to Sondra's ability to foster critical thinkers and learners than the words of her students. On my last day in this classroom, Sondra asked all of the children to write down pieces of advice that I should pass on to the preservice teachers whom I teach. Ricky wrote, "Use a lot of drama." Heather suggested, "Give children chances to give their opinions." The class gave me excellent advice—all based on their experiences with Sondra. But I found the most reflective and sage recommendation in Molly's words: "Always listen to children" (Figure 7–2). That is exactly what Sondra did.

REFERENCES

Foucault, Michel. 1972. *The Archaeology of Knowledge and the Discourse on Language*. New York: Pantheon.

Freire, Paulo. 1970. *Pedagogy of the Oppressed*. New York: Continuum.

Giroux, Henry A. 1987. "Critical Literacy and Student Experience: Donald Graves' Approach to Literacy." *Language Arts* 64, 175–181.

Giroux, Henry A., and Peter McLaren. 1986. "Teacher Education and the Politics of Engagement: The Case for Democratic Schooling." *Harvard Educational Review* 56, 213–238.

Heathcote, Dorothy, and Gavin Bolton. 1995. *Drama for Learning: Dorothy Heathcote's Mantle of the Expert Approach to Education*. Portsmouth, NH: Heinemann.

Lensmire, Timothy J. 1997. "The Teacher as Dostoevskian Novelist." *Research in the Teaching of English* 31, 367–392.

O'Neill, Cecily. 1995. *Drama Worlds*. Portsmouth, NH: Heinemann.

8

The Dilemma of the Bystander: Using Literature, Art, Drama, and Poetry to Deepen Understanding

Carmen Córdova

In the hierarchy of school curricula, the arts are ranked near the bottom. The insufficient consideration given to the arts is chiefly due to two misconceived dichotomies (Eisner 1988). The first is that art deals with the affective, while traditional curricula deal with cognition. The other is that talent and intelligence are regarded as separate. Eisner rejects both dichotomies: "The arts are cognitive activities, guided by human intelligence, that make unique forms of meaning possible" (1988, 48). One exception to arts located outside of the mainstream curriculum is literature, although many teachers still fail to view it for its aesthetic qualities. Rather, they see literature "as social documents" (Rosenblatt [1938] 1995)—thereby limiting to a narrow function the range of complex elements that are contained in literary experiences. Literature is important, Greene believes, because it helps us "realize the enormous variety of human lives" (1995, 21). Children can reinterpret their experiences and make their literary experiences conscious and self-actualizing. These opportunities are important if we are teaching for critical consciousness. Without arts in the curriculum, schools are in danger of creating students who are passive, rule-bound, and blindly obedient; we, therefore, risk that these students could become adults who "[do] not act on their freedom; they do not risk becoming different; they accede; often, they submit" (Greene 1988, 117).

124 THE DILEMMA OF THE BYSTANDER

```
                    PERPETRATOR
                         │
                         │
                         │
    BYSTANDER ◄──────────┼──────────► HERO
                         │
                         │
                         │
                       VICTIM
```

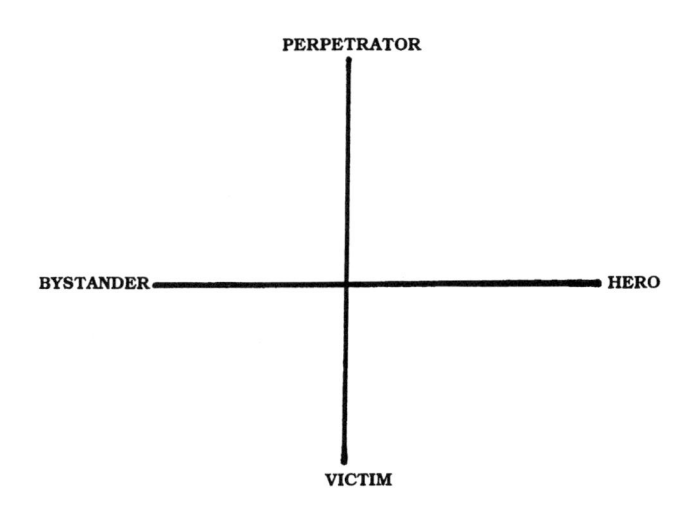

Figure 8-1: Visual representation of relationships

Our students need to be part of the solutions, and they need to be able to use what they have learned from the arts to construct theories about their moral worlds. As we make policy in classrooms and in schools, we need to listen to, value, and nurture children's insights, perceptions, experiences, solutions, and voices about their day-to-day realities inside and outside of schools. We need to allow and encourage our students to theorize as a way to become critical thinkers, to challenge the status quo, and minimize the social pain they experience in order to solve their own dilemmas. If we incorporate children's perspectives into the curriculum, we can reduce alienation and increase affirmation. Together, we can examine and deconstruct power relationships as we begin to imagine new and more humane ways of relating in our classrooms and school communities.

In order to achieve this kind of classroom, I centered the arts (including children's literature, drama, poetry, and the visual arts) in my curriculum. Through the characters and events in *The Hundred Dresses* (Estes 1944), I formulated four roles to help my fourth-graders understand the power relationships in the novel and in our classroom: perpetrator, victim, bystander, and hero. After I explained these four roles, I designed a visual representation (see Figure 8-1) to support the students' understanding. Soon, my students began to refer to these terms not only when discussing the novels we were reading, but also when analyzing power relationships in the classroom and on the playground. In the end, these four roles became central in our theory-building on morality.

EXAMINING ROLES THROUGH
THE HUNDRED DRESSES

To examine the four roles and set a moral tone in the classroom, the students and I began the year by reading Eleanor Estes's *The Hundred Dresses*. Although we considered the roles of each character, we did not explicitly label them. Instead, we discussed the characters' behaviors and feelings. In *The Hundred Dresses*, Wanda, a poor, motherless, Polish-immigrant girl, is bullied by Peggy for wearing the same faded blue dress to school every day while claiming to own a hundred dresses. The narrator, Maddie, poor herself, does not tell her best friend Peggy to stop "the dresses game" even though she feels its cruelty, for fear that she may become the next target herself. As she confides, she feels that her inaction "was just as bad as what Peggy had done. Worse, she was a coward. At least Peggy hadn't considered they were being mean, but she, Maddie, had thought they were doing wrong" (Estes 1944, 49). It is such nuances of what constitutes right or wrong behavior that provided a foundation for the theories that the students later proposed.

Not unlike many adults, the fourth-graders were unsure of Maddie's culpability in the role of bystander. During an improvised dramatization of a parent-teacher conference in class, the students' uncertainty was revealed. I paired the students and assigned them the part of Wanda's teacher, Miss Mason, or Wanda's father, Mr. Petronski. I told them to take on the role of these adults so they could have a parent-teacher conference to discuss "the dresses game."

BILLY (MISS MASON): Mr. Petronski, did Wanda say anything about the people that were making fun of her?
CHASE (MR. PETRONSKI): She said something about Peggy and um I think she said her friend Maddie wouldn't say anything, but she just stood there.
BILLY (MISS MASON): Umm, Maddie? She's a very shy girl. She doesn't talk that much. I think that Maddie might be standing around because she's afraid of what Peggy will do to her.

126 THE DILEMMA OF THE BYSTANDER

Figure 8-2: Peter's chalk drawing of Wanda

CHASE (MR. PETRONSKI): I'm more mad at Peggy.
BILLY (MISS MASON): Yeah, me too. Well, I'm very disappointed in Peggy and Maddie. (Pause) Well, Maddie didn't want to get hurt by Peggy and I know Peggy. She'd do that kind of stuff. Peggy is a very attitudinish girl.

As Miss Mason and Mr. Petronski, these students were both unwilling to indict Maddie and instead placed the blame on the "attitudinish" Peggy. In other words, it was not easy for them to define and understand the role of the bystander as clearly as they had understood the role of the perpetrator or victim. Whereas they undoubtedly knew that Peggy was at fault, they were not so sure whether Maddie had done anything wrong. They even tried to justify her behavior by calling her "shy." Their understanding of the four roles was deepened through our use of a variety of metaphors provided in the novel and from the students' own experiences.

Gardner (1999) argues that many, including experts, often privilege one form of knowing (usually math and language) at the expense of other legitimate forms. The more metaphors used, the deeper the understanding and the more children we are able to reach. The novel *The Hundred Dresses* truly resonated with my students. They could understand how

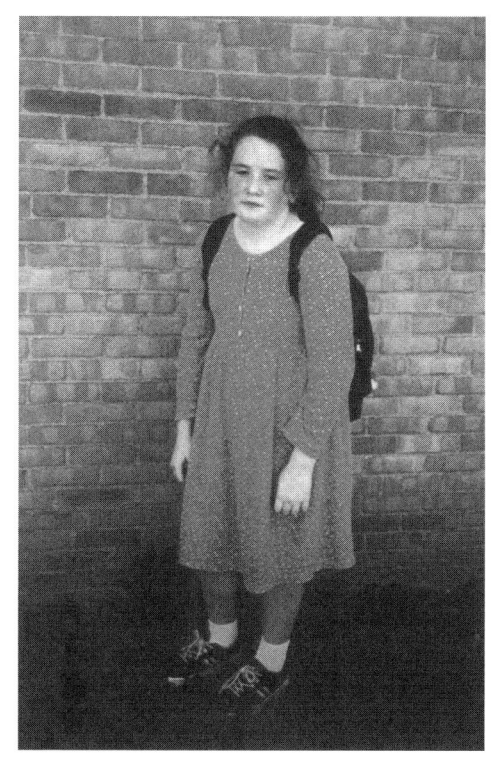

Figure 8-3: Emma posed as Wanda

the characters felt because the characters' experiences were so similar to their own experiences in school. Estes' book provided a metaphor for their experiences of alienation, pain, and bullying upon which they could build and create their own metaphors in various art forms.

As Gardner (1999) argues, any topic worth studying should be approached in many ways. Art allows many metaphors for understanding the same topic. Three of the students found a different way to represent Wanda's sense of alienation over a period of months. It was in November, very soon after we had our dramatization of a parent-teacher conference, that Peter made a chalk drawing of Wanda (Figure 8.2).

In January Oscar wrote the haiku,

Voices say ha ha.
They make life miserable
Every day, all year.

During the last week of school, months after we had finished reading *The Hundred Dresses*, Emma wore a light blue dress to school. Her classmates suggested she pose as Wanda in front of a brick wall so that I could take a picture of the tableau she created (Figure 8.3).

The children's metaphors for alienation—Oscar's haiku, Peter's chalk drawing, and Emma's tableau—each reflected their depth of understanding of Wanda's sense of isolation.

EXAMINING RIGHT AND WRONG THROUGH *SHILOH*

In Phyllis Naylor's *Shiloh* (1991), Marty (bystander) defends a beagle in a case of animal abuse. Marty witnesses Judd Travers, the abusive owner, kick Shiloh in the gut for running away. When Shiloh appears half starved and clearly mistreated, Marty cannot betray the dog and take him back to Judd, so he hides him. Marty is forced to lie to his family and friends, and in the end, after he witnesses Judd Travers poach a deer, he decides to blackmail Judd so that Judd will sell him the dog.

I used the novel *Shiloh* to help my students explore the gray areas of moral behavior. Prior to reading and discussing it in depth, most of the class viewed telling a lie in black-and-white terms: lying is wrong; honesty is good. With this book, however, the grays began to come out. I asked my students to write letters to Marty, giving him advice about Shiloh. These letters documented some of their thoughts about lying, and reflected the conflicted reactions the students had toward the idea of telling a lie. For example, Nana wrote,

> Dear Marty,
> You shouldn't have told all those lies in the first place and you wouldn't be in this mess and you would feel a lot better inside you. But since it's for one of God's creatures I would do the same thing. And also you should not have told the store man that your mom was sick. That was a huge lie. You should go back to the store man and tell him the truth and everything will be back to normal.
> From, Nana

I also invited the students to respond using visual arts, drama, and poetry so that they could further examine issues of right and wrong. The most engaging response for the children was a drama in the form of a trial with Judd (the perpetrator), Marty (the bystander and later hero), and an impartial judge who decides Shiloh's fate. I divided the class into threesomes, so that several students played the role of the judge, several others played out the role of Marty, and the rest, Judd. This format allowed every student to participate in this process drama. After everyone had a chance to play the different roles, I selected one person to embody each role and the rest of the class became a courtroom audience. After hearing two impassioned sides of the case, the judge, after much deliberation, returned the dog to Judd Travers. In the children's opinion, Judd was the rightful owner, because "he paid for it." Meanwhile, I played the role of court reporter and went from student to student with a "microphone" to solicit their reactions to the judge's decision. Most of the students agreed with the judge that Shiloh should go to Judd. However, a usually quiet girl spoke up saying, "I disagree. I think Shiloh should go to Marty. This trial isn't about money. It's about love." This statement, in fact, swayed many of the other students to change their verdict on Shiloh's fate, creating a much more caring outcome.

EXAMINING POWER STRUCTURES THROUGH *NUMBER THE STARS*

I used the third novel, Lois Lowry's *Number the Stars* (1989), to illustrate global power structures. Based on a real-life hero in the Danish resistance in World War II, Peter Neilsen, the book tells of the courage and determination of the Danish resistance as the Danes work to save the Jews from annihilation. The story is told through the friendship of two families, the Johansens (bystander) and their Jewish neighbors the Rosens (victim). The Rosens learn through their synagogue that the Nazis will soon begin to purge the capital city of Copenhagen of its Jewish population. It was with *Number the Stars*, more than the other two books, that the children realized that victims need bystanders to help confront the evil and all the power within the perpetrator.

Although we did fewer response activities for *Number the Stars*, this book helped us distinguish the power structures among the four roles. I received a memorable response when I asked the students to "write a letter to any author who had a major influence" on them, and a student wrote to the author of *Number the Stars*. Julie's letter confirmed my hopes about the depth of moral understanding that children are capable of, given the opportunity to respond to literature through art, drama, or writing, combined with their lived experience.

130   THE DILEMMA OF THE BYSTANDER

> Dear Ms. Lowry,
> Your book *Number the Stars* took my breath away. It was wonderful. I was especially interested in it because I am Jewish and I love to learn about the Holocaust and other historic events in Judaism. I was introduced to what the Holocaust was at a younger age than most children. That is mostly true because my father is a rabbi and my grandmother is a Holocaust survivor. Both of her parents were murdered in Auschwitz shortly after Hitler's army invaded Austria. My grandmother was only thirteen when this horrible tragedy occurred. I was completely horrified that only one man could carry so much power and the fact that people actually believed that by exterminating all of the Jews, the world would be a better place. I think that the diversity that we have is very important and that we should treasure it.
>
> Sincerely,
> *Julie*

Researchers discuss the ways in which knowing and knowledge are socially, culturally, and historically situated in teachers, learners, epistemologies, and curricula (Banks 1993a; Delpit 1995). However, Julie's letter actually *demonstrates* this in the way she makes a historical connection among Lowry's book, her grandmother's life as a Holocaust survivor, and her own life. As Julie expresses in her letter, she is willing to explore power structures during the Holocaust and to look at morality and power structures in her current community.

A FRAMEWORK FOR BUILDING MORAL THEORIES

The arts can deepen students' understanding and release their imagination (Greene 1995) to create more caring and just ways of being. Using the arts as a response to literature gives students an opportunity to develop a sophisticated sense of morality and to explore their own moral theories. Literature helps children find their place in the moral world. Unlike math or science, it is literature that allows students to examine the roles of perpetrator, victim, bystander, and hero.

On a daily basis, I developed students' responses to literature through drama, drawings, photos, writings, poetry, conversation, theories, and sharing their personal experiences. Some of the students' responses included chalk drawings, process dramas, a tableau, and written products. The children's visible work was displayed on panels around the room and shared collectively. Each response inspired new texts and art that deepened the students' understanding. As the students participated in reading and response activities, their responses enabled them to (1) share their lived experiences, (2) compare their lives to the fictional lives of the characters in the novels that we read, (3) examine the roles of perpetrator, victim, bystander, and hero in their own lives, and finally (4) theorize about their sense of what is "moral."

After participating in a number of reader-response activities using various modes of art, the students viewed each character's dilemma from multiple perspectives. By the end of the school year, this weaving together of reading, responding, and sharing the students' own daily experiences resulted in a cumulative theory-building.

The chart of the four roles that I devised played a central role in our search for morality. It served as a tool to help the students and me visualize the relationships among the four roles. We put the chart on a bulletin board in our classroom, and when we had finished reading and responding to the three novels, we began placing the characters from each novel on the chart. It was then that I realized that my black-and-white definitions were too simplistic. For example, I predicted that in *The Hundred Dresses*, the class would identify Maddie as a "bystander" and Wanda as a "victim." I also predicted that in *Shiloh* they would identify Marty as "hero" for standing up to Judd, his parents, and the laws to save Shiloh from further abuse. Finally, in *Number the Stars*, I felt sure that the students would react to the Nazis as "perpetrators," the Rosens as "victims," and the Johansens as "bystanders." However, I was surprised by my own naïveté and by the students' insight into the complexities of the four roles. As the students discussed where to place Marty on the chart, the notion of "hero" got complicated. Melanie described the complex and fluid nature of the hero's role. As she explained to us,

> I think Marty should stay in the middle [between hero and bystander] because he started as a bystander who became a hero and he was sometimes a perpetrator. . . . On his actual behavior, I think he should be like in the middle of bystander and victim and hero because when he saw Shiloh get hurt, it hurt him, but he didn't do anything when he saw the deer get shot. But he saved Shiloh.

As the students continued to add each character to the chart, all of the roles became complicated. It was the process of placing and moving the characters on the chart that led to the development of the children's theories.

STUDENT THEORIES ON THE MORAL DILEMMA OF THE BYSTANDER

After we had read the novels and engaged in various artistic responses, I asked my students to create a visual map of the characters in the books and their corresponding roles as victim, bystander, perpetrator, and hero. As students examined each character, we discussed the placement of a character in a certain role. The ensuing discussions revealed the students' nuanced conceptions of the characters' actions and moral development. The process of placing and moving the characters on the chart led the children to develop various theories, from which I extracted the following seven.

Theory One

A bystander who does not take action becomes a perpetrator.

Our first theory regarding the moral dilemma of the bystander came out of a discussion about where to place Marty on the chart. As Willy stated, "If you [as a bystander] don't do anything about it, you become a perpetrator because you're still letting them [the victims] get hurt."

Theory Two

For a bystander to become a hero s/he automatically falls on the bottom half of the chart where perpetrator and victim are separated.

In reference to *The Hundred Dresses*, the students had the following discussion:

> RAY: Um, as a bystander you can also become a victim because some people don't like seeing other people getting hurt. Maddie didn't like seeing Wanda get hurt so she was kinda also a victim because she didn't seeing, like some people don't like to see other people get hurt so they become victims. To take action they put themselves in other people's place. And they feel and they are kinda like a victim and they have to sacrifice themselves.
>
> CARSON: I know why they take action. Because they go to the feelings they have for them. Cause they kinda know how they feel.

Theory Three

A perpetrator can be a hero if s/he stops being mean.

Stephanie introduced the idea that Ray articulated.

STEPHANIE: Judd Travers, he got nicer at the end so maybe he can go to hero.

EMMA: I think you should move her [Peggy] a little closer to hero because she started to realize she did something wrong. She kinda reacted after Wanda moved.

GARY: They [Judd and Peggy] both did because Judd gave him [Shiloh] that collar.

LOU: He gave Marty something too, he gave him water.

RAY: Judd Travers is kind of a hero because he kind of held back his meanness when Marty was trying to be nice to him. Being a hero doesn't always mean that you save someone. It can mean changing from being mean to being nice. He went from being cruel to Marty to doing what is right.

Theory Four

Victims can be heroic if they defend themselves.

The students introduced this theory because Crystal wanted to move Wanda's placement on the chart.

CRYSTAL: I think Wanda should kinda move way up more towards hero because she ignored Peggy when they were teasing her and she didn't like let most of her crying hurt feelings show.

DEBORAH: She kinda took a risk turning all them pictures into the art contest too. She didn't know if they like them.

Likewise in reference to Shiloh, students arrived at the same conclusion about Shiloh.

DEBBIE: I think Shiloh should move kinda toward hero because you know dogs usually like to bark all the time. But when he was with Marty he hardly ever barked.

So, characters that began with victim status were moved toward hero because of how they participated in their own salvation.

Theory Five

If a victim is hurt often enough s/he will become a perpetrator.

RAY: I think Judd Travers is kind of a victim. He became mean because his dad was mean to him. He was hurt so he was kind of a victim.
MELANIE: So, Judd started out as a victim and moved up here to perpetrator.
LOU: Yeah, I think Judd was or most people who get teased a lot usually get mean.
WILLY: Also Judd's dogs, they were victims first and then they became perpetrators.

This theory about victims turning into perpetrators led to a discussion about Wanda. When I asked, "Do you think Wanda could ever become a perpetrator?" some of the students said "No." But it was Debbie who articulated the reason Wanda might succeed in breaking the cycle, leading to our next theory.

Theory Six
This cycle can be broken if the victim can forgive his/her perpetrator.

The role that forgiveness plays in this construct is critical. Early in the year, in November, when we were discussing whether it would be better for Maddie and Peggy to write a letter of apology or a friendly letter to Wanda, Billy saw the importance of forgiveness in repairing the relationship.

BILLY: Um I think it should be an apology letter because it could help her [Wanda] forgive them [Peggy and Maddie] more and it can make her feel better about herself.

Later, in May, I brought up the notion of forgiveness.

CARMEN: I think forgiveness is a big part of this whole chart we have back here, too. [Indicating the hero/bystander chart.] For example, do you think Wanda forgave her perpetrators?
CLASS: (Some yes's.)
CARMEN: Do you think Shiloh ever forgave Judd Travers?
CLASS: (Lots of chatter.)
STEPHANIE: I say Shiloh did forgive Judd Travers when Judd let Marty have Shiloh.
DEBBIE: If you do not forgive your perpetrators then will you become a perpetrator yourself.

It was in connection with this reasoning about forgiveness that the final theory emerged.

Theory Seven

Forgiveness is an act of heroism.

The topic of forgiveness did not come up again until June, during a morning sharing time when we were talking about a mother whose son was murdered while he was at a Catholic college in Ohio. She came on television and forgave her son's murderer and asked that he not get the death penalty. Carson was the main spokesperson for forgiveness.

CARMEN: When we talked about forgiveness from this chart, what does forgiving your perpetrators do? I think we talked about Wanda forgiving her perpetrators and being able to break the cycle. If you are a victim long enough, then what happens?
CARSON: I think you're really a hero yourself if you can forgive your perpetrators.
CARMEN: So forgiving your perpetrator is a heroic act?
CARSON: Yes, because it's hard to do and it requires pain and sacrifice.
BRENDEN: I don't think they [the mothers of the two murdered boys] should forgive their perpetrators cause they, they like say like those two kids, the three of them killed them and you couldn't like forgive them.
CARMEN: It would be really hard.
JASON: Why would you forgive the killers?
CARSON: I think I know the answer for Jason. So you don't have that pain in yourself. If you are a victim long enough, what becomes of you? You become a perpetrator. It's so you don't have the pain inside yourself for your entire life. If you can forgive them, it kinda goes away.

The next day, Melanie stated her position on forgiveness.

MELANIE: We were talking about some victims who grew up to be perpetrators because they were hurt but since she [Wanda] forgave Maddie and Peggy we thought that she wouldn't become a perpetrator. She forgave them so she kind of became a hero in a way.

During that same conversation, Carson spoke about the heroism of forgiveness.

CARMEN: So what is a hero?
CARSON: Someone who is a bystander and decides to take action to make things right or they could be a victim who can forgive their perpetrator.

CENTERING THE ARTS

The process through which the students arrived at these profound insights into the moral world was possible through the arts. Art enables us to look at the familiar and make it strange (Greene 1988). This is an important function if we are to help children use their art experiences to "disclose aspects of experience ordinarily never seen. Critical awareness may somehow be enhanced, as new possibilities open for reflection—it enables us to know in new ways" (131). Art, Greene continues, can make the subtle, seductive, and invisible nature of hegemonic policies visible. Art forces us to externalize our interpretations, bringing them to the public forum, empowering children "to mediate between the object world and their own consciousness, to locate themselves so that freedom can appear" (122).

Imagination and creativity play prominent roles in developing morality. "Imagination is what, above all, makes empathy possible" (Greene 1995, 3) Without empathy, Marty would not have risked saving Shiloh, and Maddie could not have felt Wanda's alienation. Children need opportunities to create and imagine hypothetical worlds where they can theorize about how their lives might be (Johnson 1993).

If students are to become autonomous thinkers, willing to challenge conventions, they need to engage in activities that promote critical dialogue about their world, ones that "enable them to imagine conditions other than those that exist or have existed" (Egan 1992, 46).

Art often is not considered part of our daily lives at home or at school. It is seen as belonging to some elite group of talented artists who get their poetry published, their paintings in museums, or their dramas onstage. Dewey (1934) describes the location of art:

> On one hand, it is assumed that there is in existence, at least in some gifted persons, an emotion that is aboriginally esthetic, and that artistic production and appreciation are the manifestations of this emotion. Such a conception is the inevitable logical counterpart of all attitudes that make art something esoteric and that relegate fine art to a realm separated by a gulf from everyday experiences. (p. 78)

Until the arts are legitimized as a way of knowing, as important tools for multiple interpretations, they will remain at the periphery of educational institutions. Gardner (1999) argues that any topic worth studying should be approached in many ways. Art allows many metaphors for understanding the same topic.

Like life in the classroom, art is at the same time affective and cognitive, individual and communal. As we get to know our students through storytelling, we must begin to introduce other art forms as well. During this particular study I might not have appreciated or understood Peter's interpretation if not for his chalk drawing of Wanda or, again, Emma's feelings without her dramatic interpretation of loneliness. The various artistic renderings of experience gave us all new insights that we could not have experienced with words alone. If we avoid privileging one form of expression over other, less traditional, art forms, then we can expect to get a fuller view of reality, enabling all of our students to achieve their full potential. Engaging children in sense-making can arouse children's imaginations. We must therefore infuse their sense-making with feelings, and their feelings with sense-making. With the arts, we can open windows to the world that were closed, locked, and boarded up.

It is the arts, with their multiple forms of expression, that make us most humane. It is therefore the arts that will enable us to explore the deep parts of our lives that only poetry, drama, song, dance, or paintings can reach. Our students are willing and able to use the arts to make meaning of our complex moral world. They are vibrant, curious, creative learners ready to share their lived experiences and blend them with others from literature, the world, and their classroom. Our students need to develop theories that not only liberate the victim, but liberate those in the role of the bystander and perpetrator as well.

REFERENCES

Banks, James A. 1993a. "The Culture Wars, Race, and Education." *National Forum* 73 (4), 39–46.

———. 1993b. "Multicultural Education: Developmental Dimensions and Challenges." *Phi Delta Kappa* 75, 22–28.

Delpit, Lisa. 1995. *Other People's Children: Cultural Conflict in the Classroom.* New York: The New Press.

Dewey, John. 1934. *Art as Experience.* New York: Perigee.

Egan, Kieran. 1992. *Imagination in Teaching and Learning.* Chicago: University of Chicago Press.

Eisner, Elliot. 1988. "Discipline-Based Art Education: Its Criticisms and Its Critics." *Art Education* 41, 7–13.

Estes, Eleanor. 1944. *The Hundred Dresses*. New York: Harcourt Brace Jovanovich.

Gardner, Howard. 1999. "Truth, Beauty, and Goodness: Education for All Human Beings." In *Teaching for Intelligence I: A Collection of Articles*, edited by B. Z. Presseisen, 27–39. Arlington Heights, IL: SkyLight.

Greene, Maxine. 1988. *The Dialectic of Freedom*. New York: Teachers College Press.

———. 1995. "Multiculturalism, Community, and the Arts." In *The Need for Story: Cultural Diversity in Classroom and Community*, edited by A. H. Dyson and C. Genishi, 11–27. Urbana, IL: National Council of Teachers of English.

———. 1999. "Art, Imagination, and School Renewal: Toward a Common Language." In *Teaching for Intelligence I: A Collection of Articles*, edited by B. Z. Presseisen, 40–53. Arlington Heights, IL: SkyLight.

Johnson, Mark. 1993. *Moral Imagination: Implications of Cognitive Science for Ethics*. Chicago: The University of Chicago Press.

Lowry, Lois. 1989. *Number the Stars*. New York: Dell Publishing.

Naylor, Phyllis Reynolds. 1991. *Shiloh*. New York: Atheneum.

Rosenblatt, Louise. [1938] 1995. *Literature as Transaction*. New York: The Modern Language Association of America.

9

Drama, Diversity, and Children: The Art and Ethics of Advocating for More than One

Beth Murray

DRAMA IN ITS ADOLESCENCE

Sometimes I imagine drama education as an adolescent at a gathering of elders. Like adolescents, our world expands as we interact with those more experienced than we are. For drama educators, education and the social sciences are like our older cousins. Theatre and the arts are like our aunts and uncles. Literature and history are like our old neighbors. Oral history and storytelling are our great-grannies. Because drama is about the human experience, almost any field could be at our gathering. Our identity emerges from this combination of influences, though it is still under construction.

We know some things about what educational drama can do, despite its relative youth. We have grown in our ability to articulate, advocate, and analyze our artistry. We have acknowledged successes and struggles in our praxis. We celebrate our roles as researchers, practitioners, artists, teachers, advocates and activists—in varying degrees and combinations. We have talented leaders and luminaries to guide and inspire us. We enjoy healthy debates with and among them. We have a growing body of literature that defines us to ourselves and others. But collectively, we remain young, our identity under construction particularly with respect to the borders of our responsibility to culture, diversity, and social justice.

This chapter seeks to both celebrate and interrogate the richness of created spaces where humanity, cultural identity, information, and artistry mingle. How do we prioritize our advocacy for drama as an art form and educational tool in relation to our responsibility to young people as reflections of and participants in our complex, diverse society? How do we balance advocacy for and responsibility to reflexive practitioners making their way through a social/political/artistic apprenticeship?

Important work has been done in this area. We have guides to help us explore culturally specific traditional literature through drama (Saldana 1995). We have works that help us examine drama through a critical lens with respect to cultural identity (Grady 2000). We have studies that describe the relationship between culture and the approaches of drama practitioners (Manley and O'Neill 1997; Garcia 2001). We have exemplars of the relationship between the theatrical, the political, and the psychological (Boal 1985, 1995, 1998). We have begun to examine how drama gets negotiated differently in different contexts. We have made steps to examine drama and its educators striving to be in-service to communities through applied theatre (Taylor 2003). We have begun, but we are still developing an understanding of the dynamic relationship between drama and diversity. Our individual and collective relationship with diversity is neither fixed in time nor uniform in character, but negotiation with it is vital to our growth. It is a rite of passage. I do not write this chapter as the mentor gently suggesting the proper path, for there are likely many—and many unknown to me. Rather I write as a questioning adolescent of my field: sometimes knowing, sometimes wondering, sometimes challenging, sometimes changing, sometimes contradicting, but always seeking growth and struggling between conformity, rebellion, and the spaces between.

We can learn from our elder fields, for they too face a similar challenge of a powerful, though often invisible, struggle. In this arena, much progress remains partially imagined, but largely unrealized. If we are to truly come of age as a field, it must be with efforts for diversity at the center, not on the margins of our collective and individual consciousness. We need to examine ourselves with respect to marginalization, representation, and genuine service.

CULTURAL BORDERS: DRAMA AND MARGINALIZATION

As a school subject and a curricular presence in North America, drama is marginalized. As a collective, we identify ourselves as being marginalized by the system of schools. Life on the margins brings with it the necessity of dualities and contradictions. We find ways to operate within the system. We seek stronger power and legitimacy within the system. Yet, we question and challenge the power structure of the system, imagining the possibilities of a revolutionized system. We often do all of these things simultaneously. With some notable exceptions, the rhetoric, policies, and paperwork of school systems allocate class time, money, and attention away from the arts, but toward more privileged/more testable subjects such as math and literacy.

As drama educators, we approach our outsider status in a number of ways. We advocate for drama as a subject deserving as much time, money, and attention as geometry and spelling receive by presenting it in the language of curriculum standards (e.g., National Theatre Standards). We advocate for drama being a useful tool across disciplines through language (Wagner 1998). We make a case for drama as a tool that belongs at the center of the curriculum to naturally foster many hard-to-accomplish curricular ideals, for it promotes integrated curriculum while framing and fostering inquiry (Heathcote and Bolton 1995) and invites the exploration of multiple perspectives while mirroring the reflexive practice of effective, ethical researchers (O'Toole 1996).

We define ourselves against dominant entities, sometimes using them to reveal who we are not, rather than who we are. By this identity, we consider ourselves to occupy the margins. We have looked to forge alliances with others on the margins. Marginalized school subjects and efforts draw our attention: inquiry, cross-curricular integration, science, social studies, literature, and art. Marginalized identity groups, both historical and current, magnetize us. We are drawn to people imbued in the tension of being outside, misrepresented, silenced—or spoken for. Some drama practitioners have firsthand experience with cultural marginality that resonates through their dramas. Others are seemingly drawn by the tension and the possibilities that drama might bring to (or take from) this tension. The nature of process drama feeds on the premise that there are margins to be explored.

Scenario I: A seventh-grade teacher notices that the social studies book she is required to use is biased to a mainstream, white-dominant, middle-class perspective. The United States Constitution is covered, but never questioned. Capitalism is explained, but there is no in-depth exploration of poverty. Her students and she both struggle to engage with the required material. She wants to use drama to help broaden, challenge, and enliven the limited perspectives provided in the text. That way, she will be making space for marginalized

voices in social studies as well as making space for the marginalized field of classroom drama. The teacher has four weeks (16 one-hour class periods) in which to work.
Questions/Challenges:

1. *Where does she start?*
2. *Does she try to capture their interest in drama first, and then follow up with research and information and exploration? Or vice versa? Or another alternative?*
3. *She really wants to help her students to begin exploring the contradictory nature and multiple perspectives of history, but knows she needs to work within the limits of her school. How does she negotiate this?*
4. *How much content does she need to know before she begins, or should she just learn right alongside the students? How much drama does she need to know? How about her students? Or should they all learn as they go?*
5. *How does the teacher's cultural identity intersect with the inquiry? How do the students' cultural identities intersect with the inquiry? What are some avenues into the work? What are some precautions?*
6. *Does anyone need to sanction or approve her effort?*

BORROWED SHOES: DRAMA AND REPRESENTATION

Getting started is a huge undertaking. The enormity broadens when we decide to use theatre (an art form in which people act as others) in combination with nonfiction/information, biographical, and real-life texts (in which real people's stories are recorded). Much of drama work relies on teacher-in-role and mantle-of-the-expert strategies, as well as other approaches adapted from theatre and the arts, as we have seen in the chapters of this book. These approaches involve the drama facilitator and the participants in exploring material and perspectives through active role creation and reflection.

If you've never seen a skilled leader of process drama work in role, try to get that experience. Words on a page help us envision steps and strategies, but there is no apprenticeship like live participant observation. Chances are, the person will also be masterful at framing participants in roles—artfully altering and challenging perspectives and presumptions. Watching teachers work skillfully with role captured my initial interest in process drama. Watching them made me want to learn how to do what they were doing. Actually, watching the teachers and the middle-school students whose attention they held and whose thoughts and voices they framed made me want to learn to do what they were doing.

The potentially contested ground of artistry, education, and cultural identity in process drama are captured in the words of Dorothy Heathcote.

> It is the nature of drama that we start exactly where we ourselves are, with our own prejudiced views. The diagnostic potential is, therefore, very valuable. I believe that classes have the same privilege as other artists in ordering and reordering their worlds, as they gain new information and experiences. (Heathcote, cited in Johnson and O'Neill 1984)

This effort to "start exactly where we ourselves are" is an important and undeniable tenet of drama work. It applies both to students and practitioner. There is no other starting place. This notion gives us the strength and courage to risk entering—and guiding others into—drama worlds (O'Neill 1995). This view helps those leading drama to strive feverishly toward understanding their students' understanding as the drama unfolds. The constructivist ideals of this tenet bind us to other disciplines resting on similar values.

Psychological Stance: Borrowing Shoes to Walk the Paths of Others

We could make a lifelong career of perfecting the way we help students work as artists "ordering and reordering" their worlds, helping them to "new information and experiences." It's a psychological notion. Much of this work rests on constructivist notions of learning (e.g., those of Vygotsky) notions of learning. Working within this perspective, teachers shift between prompting expression and challenging these individual and collective expressions with new information or perspectives.

Every moment of every drama, we are ideally participating in a reflective practice. Working in role takes time and patience and reflection to perfect. Each time I have a new group of prospective teachers working in role for the very first time, I am reminded how much risk and contradiction is required to lead from within. Drama educators must plan feverishly, yet remain open to spontaneous opportunities. We must engage through our own choices and questions, yet listen to, observe, and respond to others. We must seek and foster tension, yet remain protective of our participants. We want to guide the drama, yet give it away. It is a complex process with great rewards. Improving requires a commitment to practice over time and interrogate our weaknesses. That is not everyone's idea of a great time.

Some new teachers are naturally drawn to this sort of work. Others are not. I require them all to try it. It demands time, effort, energy, and humble reflection to begin. They all bring different strengths. Some remind me repeatedly how risky it is to work in role. Some fear looking foolish in front of their peers. Others fear "messing up" in front of me. Despite their cautious opposition, they try—publicly. Afterward, we can talk about role on a different level, with more specific detail and nuance, because now we are all wondering from inside, with a frame of reference.

Skillful drama practitioners slide in and out of centrality. They entice input, observe interaction, and then, with the group, artfully scaffold, nurture, and challenge the ideas that come forth from the group. It's beautiful to witness, but it's not where beginners begin. Beginners begin more mechanically, trying on someone else's approach—borrowing someone else's shoes, taking a walk and seeing how they work. This is part of the apprenticeship. Beginners also naturally borrow some criteria for assessment. We look outside ourselves at first. We try to read participants and observers for feedback. That is part of the art. Slowly, it becomes ours. Sometimes, however, we get so caught up in the challenge of perfecting our craft, assessing the changes in understanding within and between the students of our classrooms, that we lose sight of a larger context.

Sociological Stance: Examining Paths in Complex Context

Sometimes I have imagined observers. I'm conscious of them. They sit in my mind as I plan. They peep in the window and lurk in the back of the room as I teach. When I first started teaching, they were always students: the child I couldn't reach, the child I wanted to challenge, the class that never sat. As I moved past simply surviving and grew to know my surroundings, I would also have teachers, administrators, teacher assistants, and parents/caregivers as literal and figurative observers. While working on grant-funded projects, I'd imagine funders and administrators. During and after graduate school, I'd imagine professors, colleagues, and luminaries in the field whose work I'd only read or seen on video or the author whose book I'd used as a pretext. More recently, I try to imagine members of marginalized groups I'm intending to serve with the very work I'm doing. I'd like to explore the idea of the incidental onlooker, audience, voyeur, spy, learner, judge, artist, witness to drama—and the ethical implications of who we imagine to be just outside our windows. Beyond our immediate participants, those are the people to whom we feel most accountable in our drama work. We often claim to borrow their shoes in our dramas. Sometimes I wonder—Do we? Could we? Should we?

RITE OF PASSAGE: DRAMA'S RESPONSIBILITY TO SOCIAL JUSTICE

Every time we take on a role, we are representing someone else through ourselves. It's not just a simple game of pretend, especially when we seek to represent a marginalized individual, group, story, situation, or social condition. Taking a sociological as well as a psychological stance toward our work in drama can help us get away from the dangers of misrepresentation.

Sociology has to do with the origin, development, and structure of human societies and the behavior of individuals and groups within them. Psychology and sociology are clearly related, but sociology takes a broader view. Our scholarship has sociological undertones when we speak of critical, transformative art and education. These terms are subject to wide interpretation. Some see empathy and heightened social awareness as "transformative," while others believe transformation and emancipation should involve a social revolution both within and beyond the walls of the drama exercise. Some say the goal of drama is a change or growth in understanding. On a psychological level, this could occur whenever thinking or collective ideas shift—a psychological transformation. However, drama examined from a sociological stance requires us to examine shifting ideas and patterns among individuals and groups within a larger, layered society.

The field has embraced an array of sociocultural and critical perspectives, but we have a broad definition of what counts as "social action." When we talk of drama as a tool for social justice, we find living inspiration in the work of Augusto Boal. With his *Theatre of the Oppressed* techniques (1985) that gave way to his *Legislative Theatre* (1998), he continually examines the interplay of theatre, psychology, and politics. We study his work and priorities and choices, for he manages to account for the artistic, the therapeutic, and the political. We seek to emulate his work. Yet we are also reminded that his work has varied in response to its settings. The oppressor-oppressed relationship is different in America than it is in Brazil. It is different in different parts of America, in Canada, and among different groups within a country, with different leadership and membership and knowledge and experience (Schutzman 1994).

There is danger in equating all marginality. To whom are we accountable when we sit at the intersection of drama and marginality? How do we push ourselves toward not only examining a range of perspectives, but also examining the systems in which those perspectives operate?

Scenario II: The seventh-grade teacher decides to craft a drama/social studies unit around the inquiry: "Who is responsible for poverty in the United States?" She believes that this will allow her to pose sociological questions, prompting the exploration of various systems contributing to the uneven distribution of wealth in the United States. It could involve the Constitution as well as an examination of capitalism in human terms. The first strategy is designed to both engage students and assess prior knowledge about poverty. It begins with the machine game (participants join one by one to create an improvised, interactive, human machine), which evolves into the machine game with a poverty theme superimposed. Students are encouraged to make this an interactive sound-and-movement experience. The group reflects on patterns observed in choices made. Themes that emerge include these: poverty is a lack of money, poverty is a lack of employment, money brings power, poverty is cyclic. The following (from CRI Inline and U.S. Congressional Office of Management and Budget) is shared and discussed:

> *The gap between the rich and poor is wider than any time in nearly seventy years, with the wealth of the country's richest one percent of the population exceeding the overall possessions of the needy, who account for forty percent of the total population.*

The final strategy is an in-role meeting in which the teacher plays a member of a political action committee looking to gather press-conference questions for political candidates in the upcoming election with respect to the uneven distribution of wealth. Participants are fellow committee members. Topics generated deal with general questions, such as: "What would you do about poverty?" More specific topics include welfare, tax breaks, public awareness and stereotypes of the poor, homelessness, and equal access to education.

Questions/Challenges:

1. *What should happen next—drama, research, or a combination?*
2. *What do students know about poverty? What do they need to know?*
3. *What does the teacher know about poverty? What does she need to know?*
4. *How can she focus the inquiry without losing sociological aspects?*
5. *How can she make space for the perspectives of cultural insiders and lay the groundwork for social action?*

6. *How does she both challenge students to conduct thoughtful research with immediate relevance to their world, yet protect the same students who are more than aware of their own place in a class-conscious, capitalistic society?*
7. *Whom should she imagine to be peeping in the window as she conducts this unit?*
8. *What if she finds herself "in over her head"?*

THE TROUBLE WITH SIMPLE ADVOCACY: THEATRE AND DRAMA AS GENUINE SERVICE

Choosing to use drama as a tool for inquiry into a socially relevant, politically charged issue is a multifaceted risk.

> You are using the human condition of your students, their attitudes, their philosophy, their ideas, and you have got to use them as they really are. . . . So you are going to be involved with human material and there are some teachers not born to be involved with human material. Am I still worthy of being involved with human material is a question I have to keep asking myself. (Heathcote, cited in Johnson and O'Neill 1984, 117)

If you press Heathcote's words to also include the human condition of any group or individual on the margins whom you are intending to serve, you can see the immensity of the responsibility. Then the question stretches from "Am I still worthy of being involved with human material?" to "With whose human material am I worthy of being involved?" and "What exactly do you mean by 'involved'?"

We can, should, and do advocate for drama. But if that is our primary aim, what are we pushing? Drama and theatre by their nature require people, passion, and platform (Taylor 2003). If our passion has simply to do with the presence or absence of drama, then we are pushing a subject and strategies. We are part of the movement to make drama gain legitimacy in the schools we already know. Ideally, drama will influence the school, the school will influence drama, and it will become something else, but intertwined. However, history has shown us that in schools and other large, socially embedded institutions, change comes slowly, if at all. Drama will be no more than another passing phase bent on its own survival.

So we centralize the exploration of the human condition, rather than centralizing drama. Are we using that human condition—exploiting it to further drama, while purporting to "help"? Or are we offering drama—and by extension ourselves—in service to an idea or cause or group? Is it possible for us to be that generous? Is it possible for us to be that knowledgeable? How do we prepare ourselves to do that, if that is our aim? What happens if we aim for that and fall short? What are the possible successive approximations? What might be the damage of an approximation? Could the effort do more harm than good?

Do we follow the idea that "Imagination is more important than knowledge," as Einstein pointed out? Or do we defer to those who purport that "Knowledge is power"? If we take Einstein at his word, is it better to pretend than to know? Or have we taken the scientist's words out of context to more cleanly serve our purposes?

The dictionary says knowledge means to "possess information of facts, ideas, truths or principles"—to have clear awareness.

Imagination involves the "ability to form images and ideas in the mind, especially things never seen or never experienced directly. Is it better to envision that which is unknown, or to comprehend that which has occurred? If our teacher has students with no knowledge of poverty, is it helpful for them to simply imagine a perspective by taking on the role? Chances are the students will have a superficial knowledge of poverty that will become a stereotype in role. As teachers, are we prepared for handling this possibility in a way that respects, supports, and furthers the cause of those victimized by poverty? As teachers, are we prepared to both challenge the stereotype yet remain responsible for the emotional well-being of the students with whom we're working?

It is one thing to dismiss knowledge in favor of imagination when we possess a great deal of knowledge, as did Einstein. It is quite another thing to dismiss knowledge in favor of imagination when we possess little of it. Fold in the fact that the knowledge we're dismissing belongs to people whose history has been marginalized, and we are operating in the realm of arrogance, despite our kindest intentions. Strong drama practitioners with social justice aims provide students with frameworks for knowledgeable, informed imagination work.

Scenario III: The time the teacher allotted for her social studies/drama inquiry unit has come and gone. She needs to move on to the next unit because exams are coming up, though she is frustrated that just as she felt the class was finding a focus, the drama had to end. She decides to close with a return to the political groundwork established in the mantle-of-the-expert/pressroom strategy. She has students write in role on the eve of a political inauguration that marks a change in administration. Then she assembles students in a human hallway and employs a variation on the strategy some call "The Walls Have Ears" (see Neelands and Goode 2000). One student is selected to serve as a stakeholder in this new administration. He walks slowly down the human hallway as others give voice to thoughts and questions in the stakeholder's mind. There are insightful moments and eloquent moments. After the students leave, the teacher studies their writing more closely. She compares the in-role writing with the lists of questions she had them generate in the initial session. The topics are nearly identical . . . as is the level of depth. Despite her efforts to help students replace their psychological stance on poverty (conceptualizing it in terms of characteristics and attitudes of "poor people") with a more sociological or critical stance (conceptualizing it in terms of social systems and conditions that produce and perpetuate poverty), the former prevails. A majority of the students wrote either as the good, victimized poor person, the evil, perpetrating rich person, or the troubled politician between them.

Questions/Challenges:

1. *How could this be so, after weeks of research and drama? Did she do something wrong?*
2. *What does she do now?*
3. *What might she have done differently?*
4. *Is this "transformative education"?*

THE EASY PATH: FANTASYLAND

You can see why some people opt only to use fantasy pre-texts. There are no real histories or identities or marginalities requiring attention. That impulse is not all wrong. Fantasy is a great place to begin getting yourself and your students comfortable with using drama as a tool for inquiry. If our sole responsibility is to the participants before us, not the complex nexus of beauty and injustice beyond the walls confining our drama, it is best to linger in fantasyland. Fantasy can provide insight and exploration and even parallel reality. Most of all, it provides an opportunity for freedom from some responsibilities of representation. Fantasy, however, remains just that. Reality is messier.

COMING OF AGE: THE COMPLEX WAY OUT

Vivid drama moments come in several varieties. There are the chilling ones, during which we believe that elusive "change in understanding" is happening. The formerly silent participant speaks. The patchwork choral montage sounds like a sonnet. Five hands fly into the air during an in-role meeting, signaling, "Yes! We have achieved tension." We like to report those. We call it sharing our "best practices." And it is. But that can only be part of what we call *vivid*.

We also like to report the vivid moments that began as a struggle, but ended in success. We crave answers; getting them, giving them. We want to be part of a calculated risk that ends with hope. We share our struggles, especially if they end neatly or happily.

Occasionally, we like to humanize ourselves by reporting undeniable disasters, from which there was no recovery. We just stunk up the place. Those are vivid, too.

It is more elusive and disconcerting to articulate gnawing discomforts and contradictions, perpetual states of uncertainty. Is it me? Is it the subject matter? Is it the strategy? Is it the participants? Is it the good kind of tension that pays off later, or am I doing damage? Am I in a position to wonder? These are not vivid, isolated moments. They are states of being. We need to examine those, too. What happens when we are torn between defending drama and defending children?

What about artistic expression versus cultural overgeneralizations/stereotypes?
What about the cultural roots of our strategies?
What about the cultural identities of practitioners?
What risks do we run in allowing kids to pretend with partial information?
How do we prepare ourselves and our students to work against this?
How does drama change in response to culture? What if it doesn't?
What if the drama follows a valued cultural pattern that flies in the face of process drama core beliefs?
Are we defending drama, defending kids, defending culture, or defending rights and ideals?
What will we grow up to be as a field?
Will we even be a field?
To whom do we feel accountable?
What are we defending?

If we follow in the path of some of our elder fields, we will have some sameness and some greatness. We will keep our field central, and call on other fields to support our mode of operating in familiar patterns. We will talk of revolution, transformation, and change without really ever expecting it. We will keep ourselves in the margin. We will know only what's similar to what we've known. We will express more fervently than we receive. We will continue to gain legitimacy as an academic discipline as we continue to emulate our elder disciplines. That mission comes at a cost.

> We should not underestimate how all our acting and thinking is infected by power plays and hierarchies, and we just need to be aware of how we deal with this cultural dimension. (Rasmussen 2000)

Sometimes we cite Boal and Freire and critical theorists in the same way adolescents quote their favorite rebellious song lyrics. Critical perspectives can be poetic on the page, entrancing in the speech, and inspiring in the heart. We want to be there. We want to be a part of that rebellion. The adolescent looks in the mirror and wishes himself into the hip-hop video he just watched, borrowing poses and phrases. We read about the work of others using drama for social change and wish ourselves into similar certainty, borrowing poses and phrases. The video is finite. The book is finite. Reality is not. Videos can idealize. Books can idealize. Ideals can inform our reality in beautiful ways, but we must live our realities. And there is much work to be done.

Raising critical questions can be paralyzing work. Sometimes we are meant to stop and be still; to own our past, including our errors. Eventually, we must either move out or move on. The following is a list of advice I give to myself in places where I feel stuck. I share it with you on the chance that you may find some piece of it helpful.

1. Be an apprentice of drama. Start with fantasy to practice using drama strategies. Earn your way to reality, history, and biography, where issues of representation require more complex consideration. Return to fantasy for a change sometimes.
2. Be a student striving to be a scholar in your knowledge of any cultures, groups, or individuals you intend to explore or represent through drama. Know that not every bit of knowledge belongs in drama. Sometimes you just need to learn for yourself.
3. Remain aware of the difference between psychological and sociological inquiry. Challenge yourself to develop the sociological level, knowing that many of our very fine exemplars and strategies tend to promote more psychological analysis.
4. Make powerful, central, ongoing space for the varied voices and perspectives of cultural insiders. This implies that part of your scholarship involves building relationships across cultural lines. This also implies that you are working actively to keep the material

and the work about issues and ideas larger than yourself. Be aware of becoming accidentally central.
5. Question the literal and abstract messages of representations within and across cultural lines within your work. Continually work to establish your own critical criteria and the critical criteria of your students.
6. Examine and own your power and cultural identity. Help students to do the same.
7. Find connections to social action.
8. Expect participants' understanding of the world to include gaps, stereotypes, and misinformation for which you are responsible.
9. Participation in drama creates vivid, memorable moments. This will be true of factual, fictional, and flat-out-false information. Let facts lay the groundwork for fictional exploration.
10. Choose strategies that lend themselves to research.
11. Be wary of oversimplification into good and evil, both within the drama and in the way you view your role in relation to the material when reporting on it.
12. Revisit similar critical questions over time with the same participants.
13. Revisit similar drama strategies over time with the same participants.
14. Know why you do what you do.
15. The struggle for justice is not about you alone. It is social. There is both freedom and responsibility in approaching your work with that in mind.
16. Drama always works at the service of a human agenda. Be conscious of yours. Seek to know that of others.

REFERENCES

Boal, Augusto. 1985. *Theatre of the Oppressed*. New York: Theatre Communications Group.

———. 1995. *The Rainbow of Desire. The Boal Method of Theatre and Therapy*. London: Routledge.

———. 1998. *Legislative Theatre*. London: Routledge.

Garcia, Lorenzo. 2001. "'Finding One's Own Way' Through a Radical Critical Pedagogy." *Applied Theatre Researcher* (2), 1–10 (electronic journal of the Centre for Applied Theatre Research, Brisbane), www.gu.edu.au/center/atr.

Grady, Sharon. 2000. *Drama and Diversity: A Pluralistic Perspective for Educational Drama*. Portsmouth, NH: Heinemann.

Heathcote, Dorothy, and Gavin Bolton. 1995. *Drama for Learning: Dorothy Heathcote's Mantle of the Expert Approach to Education*. Portsmouth, NH: Heinemann.

Johnson, Liz, and Cecily O'Neill. 1984. *Dorothy Heathcote: Collected Writings on Education and Drama*. London: Hutchinson.

Manley, Anita, and Cecily O'Neill. 1997. *Dreamseekers: Creative Approaches to the African American Heritage*. Portsmouth, NH: Heinemann.

Neelands, Jonothan, and Tony Goode. 2000. *Structuring Drama Work*. Cambridge: Cambridge University Press.

O'Neill, Cecily. 1995. *Drama Worlds: A Framework for Process Drama*. New York: Heinemann.

O'Toole, John 1996. "Towards a Poetics of Drama Research." In *Researching Drama and Arts Education: Paradigms and Possibilities*, edited by P. Taylor, 132–143. London: Falmer.

Rasmussen, Bjorn. 2000. "Applied Theatre and the Power Play: An International Viewpoint." *Applied Theatre Researcher* (2), 1–10 (electronic journal of the Centre for Applied Theatre Research, Brisbane), www.griffith.edu.au/centre/cpci/atr/journal/article2_number1.htm

Saldana, Johnny. 1995. *Drama of Color: Improvisation with Multiethnic Folklore*. Portsmouth, NH: Heinemann.

Schutzman, Mady. 1994. "Brechtian Shamanism: The Political Therapy of Augusto Boal." In *Playing Boal*, edited by M. Schultzman and J. Cohen-Cruz, 137–156. New York: Routledge.

Taylor, Philip. 2003. *Applied Theatre*. Portsmouth, NH: Heinemann.

Wagner, Betty Jane. 1998. *Educational Drama and Language Arts: What Research Shows*. Portsmouth, NH: Heinemann.

Appendix: Drama and Multiple Literacy Structures and Strategies

Entering texts in multiple ways Encouraging students to interact with characters, think about who is not in the story but could be and what didn't happen but could have, and to explore opportunities for expanded storytelling and creating new texts.
Chapter 1, page 9; Chapter 4, page 62; Chapter 5, pages 72–73; Chapter 6, page 97, Chapter 8, page 125

Full circling A critical visual literacy activity to engage students in questioning, interacting, dramatizing, reflecting, and "transmediating" their understandings of a social issue.
Chapter 6, pages 89–91

Improvisation Performing spontaneous and scriptless scenes that are created entirely by a group of performing actors.
Chapter 3, page 40; Chapter 5, pages 77–82; Chapter 7, page 11, Chapter 8, pages 125, 128–129; Chapter 9, page 142

Intertextuality Consciously linking with other texts within a dramatic sequence and/or with other texts from the participants' experience.
Chapter 3, pages 40, 42; Chapter 5, page 82

Mantle of the expert Teachers or students assume a fictional role that puts students in the position of becoming "experts" or the ones "who know."
Chapter 4, page 64; Chapter 7, pages 110, 111; Chapter 9, pages 142, 146, 148

Movement Students use their bodies and movement as a form of expression or dramatic representation and to begin to gain effective and cognitive understandings of who they are in relation to others.
Chapter 1, page 9; Chapter 2, pages 20, 23, 24, 26; Chapter 7, page 109

Playmaking The process of rehearsing and presenting scenes from a play. Its focus is on bringing the story off the page, developing characters, and creating story events through blocking and dialogue.
Chapter 3, page 41

"Pre-texts" for drama Using a source that activates or provides a basis for the drama process, including a word, gesture, location, story, idea, object, image, character, or script.
Chapter 1, page 8; Chapter 2, pages 18, 19; Chapter 3, page 35; Chapter 4, page 55; Chapter 5, pages 71–72; Chapter 6, pages 92–93; Chapter 7, page 110; Chapter 8, pages 125, 128, 129; Chapter 9, page 149

Reading aloud and questioning/discussing An approach to moving into a role drama.
Chapter 1, page 8; Chapter 2, page 26; Chapter 4, page 56; Chapter 6, page 96; Chapter 8, pages 125, 128

Reading a picture or other visual media Responding to and examining visual texts to understand how messages, form, and mood are represented.
Chapter 2, page 21; Chapter 6, pages 90–91

Reflecting on drama and multiple literacy activities Students and teacher reflect on the experience and learn from it. This can be done within or at the end, through role-play, discussion, visual representations, writing, or further reading and thinking. This provides an opportunity for teachers to evaluate the success of the activities.
Chapter 2, pages 21–30; Chapter 5, pages 83–84; Chapter 6, page 101; Chapter 7, page 112

Role Dramas Creating role-playing activities with imagined roles that explore events, characters, and issues.
Chapter 3, page 40; Chapter 4, page 62; Chapter 7, pages 108, 110; Chapter 8, page 125

Script or Scene Building Working from original pre-texts and/or role dramas, scenes and scripts are developed for a play or performance.
Chapter 3, page 41

Soundscapes Interpreting images, words, mood, etc., through sequences of sound.
Chapter 2, pages 22, 24

Storyboarding and Filmmaking Turning scenes and plays into film by developing storyboards and filming scenes.
Chapter 3, page 41

Tableau A group of participants creates a "frozen picture" or image by using gesture, position, touch, expression, etc.
Chapter 1, page 8; Chapter 2, page 23; Chapter 4, page 63; Chapter 6, page 98; Chapter 7, pages 110, 112

Tapping In During a tableau or writing in role or other drama activity, a teacher may tap on a student's shoulder to ask to hear what the student is thinking or writing.
Chapter 2, page 28; Chapter 6, pages 99–100

Teacher in role Teachers enter into a dramatic role in order to invite students to enter that fictional world. Teachers use strategies such as initiating a work through a pre-text, establishing an atmosphere, modeling appropriate behaviors, moving the action forward, and challenging participants (students) from within the drama.
Chapter 1, page 8; Chapter 2, page 29; Chapter 5, pages 73, 77–82; Chapter 7, pages 110, 117; Chapter 9, pages 142, 144, 146

Theatre Games A group activity, which is limited by rules and group agreement, and which parallels the theatre experience and also the fun, spontaneity, and joy that accompanies games.
Chapter 3, page 40; Chapter 9, pages 145, 149

Visual representations Sketches, paper cutouts, or other ways for students to visually represent stories and responses.
Chapter 4, page 59; Chapter 7, pages 108–110; Chapter 8, page 127

Writing in role (and simulated journals) Students write from the imagined perspective of a character or another person in a role drama to display and extend their understandings.
Chapter 2, pages 27, 29; Chapter 3, page 43; Chapter 4, pages 61, 63; Chapter 5, pages 76, 83–84; Chapter 6, page 101; Chapter 7, pages 108–112; Chapter 9, pages 148–149

Editors

Jenifer Jasinski Schneider is an Associate Professor in Childhood Education at the University of South Florida, Tampa, where she teaches courses in literacy education and serves as the Director of the Suncoast Young Authors Celebration—a writing conference for children. Her research focuses on the study of children's writing development and effective literacy instruction, including the use of process drama and children's literature. She has articles published in *Research in the Teaching of English, Language Arts, The Reading Teacher,* and *Research in Drama Education*.

Thomas P. Crumpler received his Ph.D. from The Ohio State University in 1996. He is an Associate Professor of Reading and Literacy and Coordinator of the Doctoral Program in Curriculum and Instruction at Illinois State University where he teaches courses in educational drama and assessment of teachers at the graduate level. His work on process drama has appeared in *Research in Drama Education, The New Advocate,* and other journals. He is co-author of the book *Interactive Assessment: Teachers, Parents, and Students as Partners* (2003). His current research focuses on the role of drama in young children's writing development and the nature of validity in portfolio assessment with teachers.

Theresa Rogers is an Associate Professor in the Department of Language and Literacy Education at the University of British Columbia, Canada. She is a former high school English and Reading teacher whose research interests include the exploration of youth literacy practices from a sociocultural perspective, with a particular focus on multiple literacies, literary interpretation, and adolescent literature. She has articles published in the *Journal of Adult and Adolescent Literacy, Journal of Literacy Research, Reading Research Quarterly, and English Education*. She is co-editor of *Reading Across Culture: Teaching Literature in a Diverse Society* (Teachers College Press) and co-author of *How Porcupines Make Love III: Readers/Texts/Cultures in the Response-Based Literature Classroom* (Longman).

Contributors

Karen Kelley is an Assistant Professor in the School of Education at the University of Wisconsin-Milwaukee. Before joining UWM, she was an elementary teacher for ten years and an assistant principal for five years. She has a Ph.D. in Curriculum and Instruction from the University of South Florida. Her work as the co-director of the Tampa Bay Area Writing Project helped support her research interests in the professional development of preservice and in-service teachers in the area of writing instruction.

Trisha Wies Long is an Assistant Professor of Literacy at Cleveland State University. Currently, Dr. Long and thirteen other faculty members are working on her idea for a new graduate program for preservice, middle school teachers called Teachers for Responsive Urban Education (TRUE). She continues to incorporate critical, visual, and multiple literacies in her teaching and research, often using the full circling process as a foundation.

Carmen Medina is an Assistant Professor in the Department of Language and Literacy Education at the University of British Columbia, Canada. Her areas of interest include critical literacies, drama in education and children's literature. She is currently working on a project that examines notions of social and political embodiment through drama in critical literacy practices.

Carole Miller is an Associate Professor in the Department of Curriculum and Instruction, Faculty of Education, at the University of Victoria. She is co-author of *Learning to Teach Drama: A Case Narrative Approach* (Heinemann, 2000). Recipient of the Faculty of Education Award for Excellence in Teaching, her primary area of research is helping generalist teachers become comfortable, competent, and confident drama practitioners. She is co-author of *Into the Story: Language* *in Action through Drama* (Heinemann, 2004), awarded the Distinguished Book Award for 2005 by the American Alliance for Theatre and Education (AATE).

Juliana Saxton is Professor Emeritus in the Department of Theatre, University of Victoria. Co-author (with Norah Morgan) of *Teaching Drama: A Mind of Many Wonders* (Nelson Thornes, 1987) and *Asking Better Questions* (Pembroke, 1994), she is a recipient of the University of Victoria Alumni Teacher of Excellence award and a Public Orator for the University. She is co-author of Into the Story: *Language in Action through Drama* (Heinemann, 2004) and a recent recipient of the Campton Bell Lifetime Achievement Award from AATE.

Kari-Lynn Winters is a published academic and children's author. She is also a teacher who has taught a range of students in Canada and the United States, including pre-school, special education, primary and intermediate, high school, and now university teacher education. Kari is currently completing her coursework for her Ph.D. in the Language and Literacy Department at the University of British Columbia, Canada. Her research interests are children's literature, print literacy, and multimodal forms of learning.

Beth Murray serves as Education Coordinator for ImaginOn, where a Youth Library and a Children's Theatre share a home. She has also taught and directed in learning contexts from preschool through graduate school, working primarily through drama and literacy methods while trying to be a conscientious student of justice and equality.

Andrew Schofield is a teacher working with "at risk" designated adolescents in an inner city community in British Columbia, Canada. He has published work in the *Journal of Adolescent and Adult Literacy* and in several scholarly volumes. His interests include youth literacy, imaginative curricula, and school/community partnerships.

Carmen Córdova began her teaching career thirty years ago in Quito, Ecuador. Currently, she is a fourth-grade teacher in Worthington, Ohio, where she has taught for 17 years. Her research explores the moral development of children.